Treating the Aftermath of Sexual Abuse

Treating the Aftermath of Sexual Abuse

A Handbook for Working with Children in Care

Margaret Osmond
Duane Durham
Andrew Leggett
John Keating

CWLA Press • Washington, DC

CWLA Press is an imprint of the Child Welfare League of America, Inc. The Child Welfare League of America (CWLA) is a privately supported, nonprofit, membership-based organization committed to preserving, protecting, and promoting the well-being of all children and their families. Believing that children are our most valuable resource, CWLA, through its membership, advocates for high standards, sound public policies, and quality services for children in need and their families.

CHILD WELFARE LEAGUE OF AMERICA, INC.
440 First Street, NW, Third Floor, Washington, DC 20001–2085
E-mail: books@cwla.org

CURRENT PRINTING (last digit)
10 9 8 7 6 5 4 3 2 1

Cover design by Sarah Knipschild
Text design by Cathy Corder

Printed in the United States of America

ISBN # 0–87868–693–2

Library of Congress Cataloging-in-Publication Data
Treating the aftermath of sexual abuse   :   a handbook for working with
    children in care   /   Margaret Osmond [et al.].
        p.   cm.
    Includes bibliographical references.
    ISBN 0-87868-693-2
    1. Sexually abused children--Handbooks, manuals, etc.   2. Sexually
abused children--Mental health.   3. Child psychoanalysis.
I.   Osmond, Margaret.
RJ507.A29T74   1998   97-52025
618.92'85836--dc21

Contents

Acknowledgments

There are a number of individuals whose assistance was indispensable in putting together this book. Our heartfelt thanks go to Dr. Anita Halpern, who read each page with care and provided us with sensitive, sensible, and ultimately "do-able" advice. If errors remain in this book they are the errors of the authors and in no way the responsibility of Dr. Halpern. Her skill, knowledge, and patience with us have been a true gift.

Another benefactor has been Bill Elleker, our "research librarian" and bookseller. Bill has always taken an active interest in the development of treatment foster care. Once again he made an essential contribution by helping us find original works that translated well into the kind of practical approach we were after.

Finally we wish to thank the other members of our treatment team. While these individuals did not have the job of writing a particular chapter, their contribution to understanding the material we were gathering, helping us experiment with the concepts and techniques, and allowing us to use their work as "mini-laboratories" is truly appreciated. There are too many to list here, but we hope they do know how appreciative we are of their help.

We dedicate this handbook to Jen*. Her courage and strength, once we understood it, humbled us all. After three years of not understanding her needs, writing this book helped us to finally get it right. Thankfully we were not too late. When Jen finally began to talk, what she told us about our own work was both heartbreaking and encouraging. We hope this handbook is, in some small way, a contribution to making a safer, more responsive world for children like Jen.

M.O., D.D., A.L., J.K.
Cobourg, Ontario
October 1997

---

* The names of the children have been changed to protect their identities.

Introduction

History

After almost five years of working in a treatment foster care program, the authors of this handbook were starkly confronted with what we did *not* know about the treatment of children who were sexually abused. We were ignorant of the impact of abuse on children, the degree to which their most basic life experiences had been distorted, and the degree to which abuse affected every moment of their days. And, in light of these things, we did not know what we did not know—until the children began to teach us.

One particular case among all others stands out for us. We had worked with Jen for three years and were frustrated by the fact that she would not "talk" about her abuse, as if talking were somehow a magical cure. We believed that it was essential that Jen begin to talk about her abuse, because we felt that no real healing could begin until she had. We used various means to "get her" to talk, including a reward system whenever she had appropriate conversations with adults. Jen was the most stubborn child the team had ever come up against. She simply would not talk. Months later, we learned from the treatment center where her sister was that there was an extremely good reason for Jen not to talk. To talk meant she was risking her life. The children's father had told them he had planted a monster inside their stomach, and that if they told the secret, the monster would eat them from the inside out. When this finally came to light, Jen was able to tell us how deeply angry at us she was. We obviously had cared more about the abuse than we did her.

Eventually Jen was referred to a psychologist who was well versed in the aftermath of sexual abuse. After one or two sessions

Jen talked about her abuse, about the pressure we had inadvertently placed on her, and about all of the signs and signals we had been missing. Once this information was reported back to us, it became intolerable for us *not* to know about treating the aftermath of sexual abuse. It was this experience that led us to devise an appropriate treatment response to sexual abuse and eventually to write this book.

We became dedicated to educating ourselves; we read every article and book we could lay our hands on and retained an excellent consultant. Then we set about writing this handbook, as a way for us to organize our learning and as a way to help us teach our treatment caregivers what we were learning. As a result, this document lays out our program's approach to treating the aftermath of sexual abuse.

Treatment Foster Care

The treatment foster care (TFC) environment (sometimes known as therapeutic or specialized foster care) has a number of unique features that underpin the approach to facilitating child healing described here. TFC is a form of residential treatment where a foster caregiver, supported by a multidisciplinary clinical team (social workers, psychologists, psychiatrists), delivers therapeutic services directly.

Typically the caregiver has 24-hour access to this clinical team, whose sole purpose is to inform, guide, and supervise the foster caregiver's work. Formal clinical supervision is available at least once a week. Training is ongoing, frequent, and often quite sophisticated. Peer support plays an important role as well.

This high level of support allows the foster caregiver to carry out complex treatment plans of the sort usually seen in staff-operated or mental health-oriented residential treatment centers. The efficacy and potential of the TFC model have been well researched and described by various writers.

We designed our particular approach to treating traumatized children within the TFC model, and our approach calls for the same high level of training, supervision, and clinically rich learning environment as that model. Our clinical focus is on helping a child tell her "story." When she comes into treatment foster care, that child, like Jen, may not be able to tell her story; however, she may cue us with behaviors that hint at her story. Or, significant moments in her day-to-day life in treatment foster care may generate bits and pieces of her story. The caregivers become careful, thoughtful listeners and interpreters, so the child may come to know her own story and find the path to healing.

This method involves treatment that is carried out in the child's day-to-day living environment by a sensitive and well-trained therapeutic foster caregiver who offers guidance to the child. We view other forms of treatment as supplemental, not central, to the child's progress. Our experience using this model in the TFC environment suggests that foster caregivers can reliably assist severely traumatized children, with sometimes quite remarkable results. To illustrate how our approach may be applied in the "real world," we have included throughout the text vignettes of children's experiences in treatment foster care.

It should be noted, though, that this material is not limited in its application to the TFC environment alone. This information has been well received by other adult caregivers living with traumatized children and by the support staff that surrounds them. In Ontario, Canada, we have used the material to train police officials, child welfare workers, and individuals working in residential treatment settings other than TFC.

We have, however, found the material is particularly applicable to foster caregivers in traditional fostering environments, especially as we work toward a collective vision of all foster care being conducted in a professional, clinically oriented team environment. For this group, agency follow-up and access to competent, ongoing consultation is an important ingredient in ensuring appropriate implementation of the ideas described here.

Limitations

This book is not written by experts in treating the aftermath of child sexual abuse, nor is it meant to provide definitive training. It is simply a review of what we ourselves found useful in our studies and is offered as a beginning point for our colleagues who are engaged in the same struggle we found ourselves in with this population. We hope it will give the reader access to more knowledge than we had when we were first responsible for treating these children.

As you read through this handbook you will note a few things. First, as much as possible, we have tried to keep the language simple and easy to understand. We did it for ourselves. We felt that if we could explain it clearly and simply, then we had understood it well enough. Second, for easy readability, there are few footnotes or references throughout the book. We have reviewed the literature for you and reported on what we found to be practical, useful information. We simplified and summarized this information to be as true to the original meaning as we were able and still retain a hands-on focus. Finally, we also want to make it clear that much of the material in this book is not original work. The work on which we based our thinking is all listed in the recommended reading lists at the end of the chapters and the bibliography. We highly recommend that readers pursue their learning by reading the original works.

Training Suggestions

Over the past four years, we have had the opportunity to regularly use this material in training sessions in diverse settings. We experimented with various formats, group sizes, handout styles, etc., and finally settled on a relatively simple approach to training others, which is summarized here. An outline for our three-day training workshop can be found in Appendix A.

The goal of our workshop is to empower caregivers to better understand the issues and respond with more sensitivity to the children in their care. Improved child advocacy is a secondary goal. Learners should already have some basic training in child abuse, its detection and investigation, family and child development, and a basic understanding of the impacts of abuse. With those learner qualifications, trainers can then use this handbook as the basis for a training workshop that consists of the following sessions:
- Reviewing basic information about the nature and progression of child sexual abuse;
- Understanding the impact of abuse and trauma on the child's presentation, development, and functioning;
- Developing a way of discovering and exploring the child's "story" and working with the child to uncover the impacts;

- Demystifying "treatment" and providing guidelines for choosing the appropriate treatment format;
- Reviewing the goals of treatment and describing a process for meeting them within a therapeutic milieu; and
- Reviewing the tasks and skills necessary to help children in their daily living environment.

A two- or three-day workshop with a group of about 20 seems to be the optimal format for such training. That size allows us to "work" the group and facilitates active discussion, which is not practical with larger group sizes. Smaller groups can be too intimate for the emotional impact this material tends to provoke. Invariably, trainees will become overwhelmed with emotion as they struggle with the new knowledge that they have responded to a behavior with anger, frustration, and a desire to control the behavior, when that behavior was actually an attempt by the child to communicate. Group members should be warned these feelings might emerge and that this reaction is typical. A group of about 20 allows some anonymity as the struggle with these feelings continues.

During discussion sessions, we use overhead summary slides of the material as a guideline. We also use cases from our practice to highlight parts of the material and to serve as practice examples. Trainees often have excellent examples (or truly puzzling cases) that add to the discussion.

The trainer must be comfortable with the topic matter. A teaching style that models the use of humor as a tool, honest self-reflection, acceptance of mistakes made, and the motivation to "do better" seems to be effective. We developed the skill to work comfortably with sample cases from the participants later, as our own expertise with this child population grew.

We have experimented with various handout and workbook formats, but overwhelmed trainees demanded to have the whole handbook, which always led to some late-hour photocopying. We now give the handbook out as a matter of course. The feedback seems to be that the book allows participants to recreate the same energy of new insights and discoveries in their own environments once the training session is over.

Feedback also suggests that reading the handbook without some form of group exploration is a much less rich learning opportunity. If no trainer is available, participants may benefit from reading the handbook as part of a group exercise. For example, several evening training sessions could focus on a chapter per evening. A facilitator could guide discussion on what learners feel the material means to them and pull out case examples from the group's practice to examine the concepts under discussion. Our own training began that way, before we had developed the in-house expertise to teach confidently.

Note: In the handbook, "she" is used when discussing the victim, caregivers, and other therapists. This choice of pronoun is in no way reflective of who this material applies to. As many males as females have benefited from the material in this book. "She" may be taken to mean "he" in all instances.

Recommended Reading

Foster Family-Based Treatment Association. (1995). *Program standards for treatment foster care.* New York: Author.

Hawkins, R. P., & Breiling, J. (1989). *Therapeutic foster care: Critical issues.* Washington, DC: Child Welfare League of America.

Meadowcroft, P., Tomlinson, B., & Chamberlain, P. (1994). Treatment foster care services: A research agenda for child welfare. *Child Welfare, 73,* 565–583.

Meadowcroft, P., & Trout, B. A. (1990). *Troubled youth in treatment homes: A handbook of therapeutic foster care.* Washington, DC: Child Welfare League of America.

Osmond, M., & Dorosh, M. E. (1992). The tri-CAS treatment foster care program: A summary of findings in a pilot project. *Ontario Association of Children's Aid Societies Journal, 39,* 18–20.

1 The Impact of Sexual Abuse on Children

Understanding the Sexually Abused Child in Foster Care

A child who comes to foster care brings with her a host of experiences, many of them frightening, bewildering, and upsetting. Often we do not know much about this child when she comes into our foster homes and child care settings. She may have told just enough of her personal story of abuse and trauma to be removed from home, but the details of what she has lived through are still a mystery.

The child's behaviors tell her story every day, through a variety of tiny clues and cues. When we are careful observers, these behaviors will form a pattern that can tell us something about the child's experiences. Eventually, by understanding the meaning of the behaviors and responding sensitively, we can unlock the mystery of the child's experience. If we are responsive to the clues and cues the child gives, we may be able to form the kind of relationship that allows us to guide her to a path of healing.

This process is known by many names: "helping," "treatment," or "advocacy" being some of them. Whatever the term, the process begins when the caregiving adult has a good sense of the impact of abuse on a child. When the child presents one of the behaviors that typically result from abuse, the caregiver is able to recognize that behavior as a clue to how the child has been hurt by her abuse experience. The adult can then respond in a way that is sensitive, supportive, and helpful.

This requires a solid grasp of what typically happens to a child who has been abused. For instance, what was the abuser like? How did the abuse probably progress? What experiences surrounded the abuse, which may have contributed to the child's thoughts and feelings about the abuse? How is a child affected by abuse, psychologically, developmentally, behaviorally? This chapter addresses these questions. We will look at how and why abuse happens, typical psychological effects of abuse, and characteristic child behaviors and relationship problems.

Finally, we will review the "normal" physical, cognitive, and social/emotional development of children and contrast this to the developmental problems often seen in children who have experienced trauma through sexual abuse, physical abuse, or severe neglect or emotional abuse. This information is the foundation of the knowledge that the caregiver can rely on in the day-to-day work with the child.

Definition of Sexual Abuse

Sexual abuse may be defined as any inappropriate sexual contact between a child and a person or persons who have power or control over the child; this person(s) may or may not have used force. Sexual abuse perpetrated by a family member is called *intrafamilial abuse*. Perpetration by immediate family members (e.g., mother, father, brother, sister) is usually referred to as *incest*. Sexual abuse perpetrated by an individual outside the family (e.g., teacher, club leader, neighbor) who has power is known as *extrafamilial abuse*.

Why Abuse Happens

There are four conditions that predispose the occurrence of abuse and that are always present when a child is being sexually abused:
- An individual who has sexual feelings toward children is present.
- This individual does not have well-developed *internal inhibitors* (the ability to recognize that a feeling or behavior is wrong, to regulate the sexual feelings, and to control the behaviors).
- There are no *external inhibitors* (forces outside of the adult which will label the sexual feelings inappropriate, cause the sexual feelings to be regulated, or prevent the feelings from being acted on). Alternatively, the external inhibitors have been successfully circumvented.
- A vulnerable child is present.

How Abuse Happens

While abuse can begin at any time and does not follow an invariable progression, researchers have identified a rough pattern, or sequence, of abusive behaviors[1]:

- Inappropriate nudity ("parading around") or forcing child to observe sexual activity;
- Inappropriate sexual talk (sexual indoctrination of the child);
- Forcing a child to expose her own genitals;
- Forcing a child to fondle adult genitals;
- Fondling a child's genitals over, then under, her clothes;
- Forcing a child to perform oral sex on adults, either fellatio or cunnilingus;
- Adult performance of oral sex on the child;
- Digital penetration of the child's anus;
- Digital penetration of the child's vagina;
- Penetration of the child's vagina or anus with foreign objects;
- Penile penetration of the child; and
- Sexual mutilation or torture.

The sequence can take many years to fully unfold, or, in the case of a vulnerable child, can progress within a matter of weeks. Not all sexual abuse reaches penetration. Steps 1 through 4 may be seen as just as abusive as steps 5 through 7. The level of trauma experienced by the individual child is what defines "badly abused" in any given case, not necessarily the actual events of the abuse.

Understanding the Abuse

The following information is extremely important for the caregiver to know—not only to understand the child's world but also to understand which of our own inadvertent behaviors may act as reminders, or triggers, of the abuse. Some of these details will be contained in the investigation reports, some are known by previous caregivers or therapists, and some will unfold as we work with the child. These nine key items help us to understand each child's case in order to individually tailor treatment.

---

1. Adapted with the permission of The Free Press, a division of Simon & Schuster, from *Handbook of clinical intervention in sexual abuse* by Suzanne M. Sgroi, M.D. © 1982 by Lexington Books.

S even-year-old Sally told only enough of her story to the child protection worker to get the abuse to stop. She didn't mean for charges to be filed or to be taken away from home. She just wanted him to stop. She told the worker that he had touched her sexually. The worker could not know that he had been penetrating her vagina with his fingers and her toys since Sally was quite young, and that she had finally told when he informed her she was getting big enough for intercourse. The worker did not ask about the climate of sexual indoctrination that had happened before the disclosed event. The rest of Sally's story began to unfold when her treatment foster mother's elderly father came to visit, and Sally began to take off her clothes. When foster mother responded, "Sally, you are taking your clothes off. Why is that?"

Sally explained "That's the rules. Whenever Grampa comes over, all of the children must be naked. Mummy too."

---

1. **Who was the abuser?** What relationship did this person have with the child? How did the child feel about the abuser, both before and after the abuse? What are the positive and negative feelings the child has towards the abuser? (**Note:** Both kinds of feelings will be present).

2. **What type of abuse occurred?** Looking at the sequence on page 9, where was the abuser on the continuum? What was likely to have happened next?

3. **Where did the abuse occur?** Was it in the child's room or the bathroom (the two most common settings)? Was it in the car or the parent's room? Where else? What might the child feel about any of these places?

4. **When did the abuse take place?** Was it always at bedtime? Was it on Saturday morning when Mother went grocery shopping? Was it part of "special drives" in the country to give Mom a break on Sunday mornings? How will the child be feeling at any of these times? How old was the child when it began? When it stopped?

5. **How did the abuse occur?** How did the child know it was time for the abuse to start? What was said to the child? How did the abuse progress? What were the smells, sounds, tastes, colors, etc., that the child came to associate with the experience?

6. **Was silencing the child an important part of the abuse?** How did the abuser ensure that the child would not tell? Did the abuser use violence? Did the abuser tell the child something about her body? Did the abuser tell her that something might happen to someone else? What did this child believe would happen if she told, and how much did she think she was risking by telling?

7. **What other disclosure issues are important?** Why did the child feel compelled to disclose? What happened after she disclosed? How did she feel about it? How did the perpetrator react? How did her family react? How did the police, the child protection agency, her friends, etc., react? How was her life, and that of her family, disrupted? How does she feel about that?

8. **Other special circumstances may be present** that would need to be dealt with before any other work can begin, such as the following:

   • The child suffers acutely from the aftermath of severe neglect, family chaos, or physical abuse. The sexual abuse plays a lesser role in terms of the child's immediate needs.

   • A significant health issue has emerged, such as pregnancy, venereal disease, internal scarring, etc.

   • The child is in a constant state of anxiety and worry about her future and/or her physical and emotional safety.

   • The perpetrator has become ill or died (perhaps as a result of suicide), leaving the child to cope with her personal response.

   • A court order, or the child's inability to stop having contact with the perpetrator, has lead to regular access arrangements with the perpetrator. The emotional effects of such contact may be significant. In cases where extensive indoctrination is in place, seemingly innocent contact can be loaded with sexual suggestion, controls, and rituals associated with the abuse, despite the presence of a supervising person.

   • The child's emotional state and feelings around sexuality generally are highly ambivalent. For instance, the child may have felt sexual towards the adult. The child may have experienced the abuse as the only time she could feel close. In the case of a boy, he may have felt aroused by a homosexual encounter and worry about what this means.

L ittle information was available about Carlie when she came to the foster home. There were vague indicators of abuse, but nothing clear. It was still too early to really know her. A few weeks into the placement, the foster mother had to go to an agency meeting. Her husband agreed to do Carlie's bedtime. At bedtime, the foster father asked Carlie to put on her pajamas and brush her teeth: "Bring the brush in here and I'll do your hair." When Carlie was ready she stood in the living room and whispered "I'm ready." The foster father felt there was something wrong, but he could not put his finger on the problem.

When he had brushed her hair, he took Carlie by the hand, led her to her room, tucked her in, kissed her on the forehead, and said goodnight. The next day Carlie complained to her worker that she had been sexually abused by her foster father.

The worker was visibly upset when she interviewed the foster father. "I didn't think it was important to tell you. When Carlie was abused by her father, he had her put on pajamas and he brushed her hair. Then he took her to bed and started to abuse her." For Carlie, there was no real difference between what her father had done and what the foster father did.

---

9. **Protective factors** are what the child had available to her to help her survive and might include a special relationship with a teacher, the personal strength that allowed the child to refuse to act as a compliant victim, or a particularly well-done abuse investigation and subsequent therapeutic intervention.

The Impacts of Abuse on the Child

The abused child has deep and lasting scars. Those scars can be both psychological and behavioral. The scars are what bring the child to treatment and what prevent her from getting on with her life. This section provides a brief summary of the effects of sexual abuse on a child—psychologically, behaviorally and relationally, and developmentally.

Psychological Effects

In this section we will look more closely at some of the impacts associated with abuse that are psychological in nature:
*   Posttraumatic Stress Disorder (PTSD),
*   Distortions in thinking and beliefs,

- Emotional problems, and
- Personality and self-esteem problems.

These are the ways that children initially react to trauma, protect themselves from the impact of trauma, and continue to show the effects of trauma.

Posttraumatic Stress Disorder

Terror disrupts the normal functioning of a child's brain, and resulting changes in the brain's chemistry cause a sensitivity to adrenaline. For some time after the traumatic event, when a child experiences an increase in excitement, stress, or even pleasure (which leads to a normal increase in adrenaline) she reacts as if she were in danger. During these times, she may feel as if she were reexperiencing the traumatic events of the past. This is so distressing that the child actively avoids any stimulus she has come to associate with the trauma. The characteristic symptoms of PTSD are described below.

Flashbacks—sudden intrusive sensory memories, such as seeing the image of the abuser's face or hearing the abuser's voice making obscene or abusive statements. The child may experience choking sensations related to forced oral intercourse, remember the taste of semen, the smell of the molester's alcohol-laden breath, or the feel of hands grabbing genitals, legs, or thighs. These flashbacks are as strong and real as if the event were happening in the here and now.

Flashbacks cause the child to feel bizarre and out-of-control. They can be triggered by abuse-related events or stimuli (sound, smell, color, people, patterns of events); sexual interactions (interactions with a sexual tone or content, either pleasant or frightening); telling the story of the abuse; reading about or seeing violence; or even sexual activities (petting, fondling, sexual intercourse, viewing pornography, nudity, etc.).

Sleep Disturbance—Sleeping patterns are always particularly vulnerable to stress, especially for traumatized children. While not necessarily a sign of trauma, intrusive memories can occur during sleep in the form of frequent and intense nightmares, night terrors, and sleepwalking, experiences that can disrupt sleep. Children may also have difficulty falling or staying asleep, they may wake up early, or they may sleep late in the mornings after a fitful night.

F rom time to time, 12-year-old Amy received reports from her worker on her parents, who were in prison. These reports were important to her; as long as she knew they were both in prison, they could not hurt her. Unfortunately, news of her parents acted as a trigger for flashbacks that occurred at bedtime.

Her bed became the visual stimulus for a host of sensations and tactile memories of abuse perpetrated by both her mother and her father. The worst image of all was the sensation of her father inserting a gun into her vagina and threatening to shoot her there if she told. When these sensations became overwhelming, frail little Amy had the strength to rip the mattress from her bed and attempt to shove it down the basement steps.

Her foster mother, who had no idea what was happening, found herself struggling to prevent the child from ruining the mattress. Time after time they ended up in a major power struggle, and Amy eventually became violent with her foster mother. Finally, the placement broke down, and Amy came to treatment foster care.

There appear to be two types of nightmares. The first tends to happen more closely after the traumatic event; the child experiences real and graphic images of the actual traumatizing event. These tend to decrease over time. The second type of nightmare tends to persist longer and involves themes of intrusion, danger, or violation.

Night terrors are episodes of extreme terror, from which the child cannot be aroused. The child will look terrified and scream or act in a panicked, uncontrolled fashion. When night terrors finally end, the child will relax and fall into a peaceful sleep; she will typically not be able to remember the terrors the next morning.

Sleepwalking (night wandering in a partially awake state) is another common sleep problem for traumatized children. The child may get up in the night and wander around the house with a blank stare. The child seems unaware of her surroundings, and when someone speaks to her, she will respond in a somewhat dazed fashion.

Automatic Arousal—a constant state of being "on alert." The child may appear fidgety, jumpy, or tense, or will flinch at the slightest hint of danger. Sometimes these behaviors result from anxiety. Sometimes the child's mind generates them to keep her distracted from abuse-related thoughts. And sometimes they result from the child's overwhelming, intrusive thoughts of being violent or out of control.

Cognitive Distortions

In an effort to make sense of the traumatizing events in her life, the child finds or creates cause/effect relationships in the events surrounding the abuse. She perceives, interprets, and draws conclusions based on her developmental level and her understanding of how the world operates. As a result, she makes connections that would normally not be made. These *cognitive distortions* affect her view of the world around her.

She may believe that anything bad was caused by something within herself. She may feel helpless and in chronic danger. She assumes she never has any options and can never do anything to correct a situation. She is passive and has learned to feel and behave helplessly.

Sometimes a child who has been abused is *hypervigilant*, or constantly on guard for danger. This child cannot relax and settle into relationships. She is sure at any moment the relationship will turn and become dangerous. An adult caregiver's warm and nurturing behaviors are perceived as set-ups for future abuse. There is no such thing as trust.

On the other hand, the abused child may exhibit a complete lack of caution. She may put herself at risk constantly, do dangerous things, or be prone to accidents. She does not intentionally cause her frequent injuries, but they are a reenactment of how she expects to be hurt in her world.

She may feel like such a failure that she believes everything she is involved with is guaranteed to turn out badly. If she is doomed to fail, why try? She will avoid challenges, procrastinate, purposely underachieve, and it will all make sense to her if she believes she will fail.

An abused child is often preoccupied with control, because control has come to mean survival. Even a small loss of self-protection could lead to a catastrophe. Sometimes noncompliance is not noncompliance at all, but a desperate attempt on the child's part to maintain control over her environment. The child believes giving control up even to the caring adult could put her in grave danger.

J ay's father liked to dress up in black robes and take his five children into the graveyard at night. There he would perform various ritual acts that ended in sexual torture for the children. Before we knew this, Jay gave us clues with his behavior. If he saw an adult dressed in black, he would exhibit extreme anxiety, and soon afterwards he would engage in some kind of control battle with his treatment parent. Car rides at night could always be counted on to lead to an episode of total noncompliance. It took many months, and a great deal of sensitive encouragement, before Jay could tell us his belief: black clothes and nighttime trips were a signal that abuse was about to occur.

She is likely to misinterpret the intentions of others. She will think, "Haven't I been right to be suspicious of kindness in the past?" She will interpret as dangerous things that may seem neutral or positive.

The cognitive processes of a sexually abused child are quite primitive and often lead her to the wrong conclusion. Her line of thinking may go as follows: "I am being hurt. My parent is doing it either because I am bad or because they are bad. Adults hurt children for 'their own good,' therefore it must be my fault I am being hurt. Therefore, I am as bad as what is being done to me. The punishment fits the crime. I am hurt often and deeply, so I must be very bad."

The result of this cycle of thinking, as you can imagine, is a deep self-loathing. The degree to which these children hate themselves is startling, once you have been allowed to have a glimpse of it, and caregivers will find it difficult to help the child overcome self-loathing.

Emotional Difficulties

Most children find emotional situations challenging and confusing. As they develop normally with the help of supportive adults, they are able to cope with difficult times. Children who have suffered traumatizing abuse, however, will have problems dealing with heightened feelings. Often abused children have difficulty identifying, expressing, and sorting through any emotions, not just those brought about by the abuse. Traumatized children may develop emotional problems, including depression, anxiety, sexual dysfunction, somatization, and emotional regulation difficulties.

Depression—chronic sadness, unhappiness, low self-esteem, self-blame, and perceived helplessness. Depression is associated with self-hatred and may lead to such behaviors as numbing, self-mutilation, and suicidal ideation.

Anxiety—feelings of general vulnerability and susceptibility to violation. The anxious child has not had an undisrupted, secure attachment to a primary caregiver; more likely she had an insecure or anxious attachment or felt abandoned. As a result, the child may be angry, avoidant, and distressed when she is involved in "nurturing" relationships, either with her own or substitute caregivers. This child will have an exaggerated response to anything that feels like abandonment.

Sexual dysfunction—All children develop sexually, just as they do emotionally, physically, and socially. The abused child's normal sexual development has been disrupted. A traumatized child may develop a host of difficulties in the area of sexual functioning, because she is precociously sexually aware, often physiologically aroused, and she has had sexual experiences that she is developmentally unable to make sense of.

A *sexually reactive* child is often sexually overstimulated. She displays more sexual behaviors than her age peers, such as heightened interest in sexuality, masturbation, and touching other children in a sexual way. Shame, guilt, and anxiety may accompany these behaviors.

Some children become involved with *extensive mutual sexual behaviors* with their peers, although this activity is not coerced or hostile. The child's attitude toward these sexual behaviors is matter-of-fact; sexuality has become a way of making the most basic of human connections in the absence of other relationship skills.

Children who molest seek out children and coerce them to be involved in sexual activities through bribes, threats, or manipulation. These children are unable to recognize the feelings of or empathize with their victims, because their sexual behavior is tied up with anger, anxiety, and confusion about sexuality.

Sexually active teens might struggle with reduced arousal, extreme muscle tension, frightening flashbacks, or pain in the genital area during intercourse. Alternatively, they might establish a form of closeness without intimacy through sexual promiscuity or prostitution.

At 14, Mitzie had a history of several arthritic crises that caused her to be admitted to the hospital for extended rehabilitation stays. During her last admission, her physician decided that surgery was necessary. Mitzie was prepped and anesthetized. When she was being placed on the operating table, however, her doctors noticed something remarkable. While Mitzie was unconscious, there was absolutely no sign that her joints were arthritic. When she awoke, the arthritic-looking joints reappeared. Mitzie's burden of secrets and anxieties was the cause of her physical problem.

Somatization—difficult emotions are physically internalized, and the body then reacts with such symptoms as stomachaches, headaches, nausea, sleep disturbance, anorexia, muscle tension, or high blood pressure. Frequently these symptoms are associated with anxiety.

Difficulty regulating emotions—displays of emotions that are either exaggerated or played down. We have all met children whose responses are "too big" or "too little" for the circumstances. These extreme emotions can be centered around deep feelings of rejection, betrayal, and abandonment. These deep, strong feelings make it hard for children to respond to emotional events in a more "regulated" way.

Dissociation—a normal psychological defense that human beings use in the face of stress. We separate ourselves emotionally from an event so that afterwards we cannot recall the pain that went with it. Examples of dissociation might include momentary blanking out when we become overwhelmed, or "cutting off" our ability to remember troubling events. (The classic example is the forgotten pain of childbirth.) Dissociation falls along the following continuum, depending on the amount of pain involved or the severity of the event that the mind is trying to defend itself against:

- *Disengagement*—the child separates herself, or "spaces out," from the stressful event by withdrawing into an emotionally neutral place. She places her thoughts and feelings on hold. This can last from seconds to several minutes and can happen several times a day.
- *Detachment/Numbing*—the child removes herself from her own feelings as a defense against the pain. The detachment can be-

come generalized, so that the child has difficulty feeling anything at all or is unaware of the feelings. This often happens in
therapy sessions when the child feels a need to protect herself
against great pain.

- *Observation*—feeling separated from one's body. The child experiences herself as "watching" the events in which she is involved and not directly participating.

- *Amnesia*—the child may suffer from repressed memory of specific events or short- and long-term memory loss in general. The
  traumatizing event has been banished from the child's awareness. Such severe maltreatment as torture can be repressed in
  this way.

- *Dissociative Personality Disorder*—also known as multiple personality disorder or the development of separate personalities.
  This disorder is relatively rare and is the ultimate dissociation.
  It usually occurs as a result of particularly cruel or sadistic abuse.
  The child lets only a small aspect of her awareness be present for
  the abuse. She organizes her emotional life so that the whole
  personality is made into little "compartments." Each compart-
  ment holds memories, feelings, worries, etc., that were overwhelming for the child.

  Over time, these compartments may take on the aspects of
  alternate selves, with their own names, ages, memories, and
  tasks. None of these "selves" communicate with each other, and
  a separate "self" handles each problem. The child often feels
  confused if she cannot remember whole periods when another
  "self" has been functioning. Successful treatment results in the
  child accepting all of the "selves" she has created to protect herself as equally important and valuable, understanding that these
  selves are in fact parts of her, reintegrating all of the selves, and
  learning to allow her whole self to respond to life's events.

Personality and Self-Esteem Problems

Establishing a sense of "self" in a child is important to her ongoing development as a secure, competent individual. Children with
well-developed personal identities have personal defenses and coping strategies that are sufficiently developed to deal with day-to-

B ill's treatment parents began to suspect that something beyond simple manipulation was going on when he began to complain about "Jason" trashing his room. When Bill was disciplined for destructive behavior and asked to clean the room, he complained sincerely and heartbreakingly about the unfairness of it all. It was Jason who had done the damage! But there was no Jason in the house.

The mystery was "solved" when, as part of a routine psychological assessment, the psychologist discovered that Bill was developing second and third personalities. These "children" were able to express the emotions Bill could not. "Jason" housed deep rage and wasn't afraid to show it. "Amanda" was tender and vulnerable and wanted to be cared for.

Next time Bill complained about having to clean up Jason's mess, the treatment parent responded by saying "Look, you all did it. You, Jason, and whoever else, need to get in there and clean up that room!" Bill stopped complaining about unfairness when confronted by this simple, inescapable truth.

---

day problems and anxieties. These children are able to grow, learn, participate, produce, and enjoy. They have a sense of how they influence others, how they themselves are influenced, their own likes and preferences, and their place in the world.

A child without a well-developed sense of self might invest most of her energy in containing anxiety, leaving little left for investment in growth. She might be overwhelmed by anxiety that her personal defenses cannot cope with, leading to a variety of anxiety-based behavioral problems. This child might be confused about her identity. Is she worthwhile? Does what she want or believe have value? Does she have choices? Is she good, bad, a victim? Why do some people tell her one thing about herself, while the abuse experience suggests the opposite? Who is she, and how does she relate to others?

This lack of a sense of self will result in difficulty recognizing appropriate boundaries and feelings of personal emptiness. The child will also have trouble fully experiencing the personalities of others. Instead, she has limited awareness of those around her except in terms of how they impact on her own needs. An abused child is often unable to find internal resources for comforting or "soothing" herself.

Behavioral Effects

Other problems may include disturbances of relatedness or intimacy, altered sexuality, adversarial or manipulative behaviors, suicidal or parasuicidal gestures, running behaviors, aggression, avoidance behaviors, tension-reduction behaviors, and codependency. These behaviors affect the child's ability to enjoy healthy relationships with others.

Disturbed relatedness—the child's ability to experience positive relationships has been compromised. She feels distrust, anger, fear of those with greater power, and perceptions of injustice. Some children might be too inclined to respond to the demands of others at their own expense. This is called *accommodation*. Accommodation responses might include avoidance, sexualization, adversarial behavior, or attempts at ingratiation.

Intimacy disturbance—the child feels ambivalence or mistrust about interpersonal closeness. She has trouble forming and sustaining close interpersonal relationships. She easily overreacts to perceived rejections and tones of conflict in relationships and has difficulty with trust, one of the basic elements of a truly intimate relationship.

The child may have identified closeness and nurturing with sex, especially when the abuser was the more nurturing parent and the nonoffending parent was psychologically absent. When the child was romanced or wooed by her abuser, she may have come to see herself as an equal and willing participant, leading to intense guilt and self-loathing later on.

Altered sexuality—normal sexual functioning is impossible. The child's introduction to sexual behavior told her that such behavior is an abusive interaction, and this experience will have varied impacts on her sexual self (identity). Those impacts might include the following:

- Sexual dysfunction related to fears of revictimization;
- General distrust of sexual partners;
- Tendency, despite fear, to be dependent on or overidealize partners;
- Preoccupation with sexual thoughts, tendency to sexualize ordinary relationships;

J ade was new to the school. She wanted to make a new
friend. So she went up to the little boy she had her eye on all
day and said, "Hi, want to do sex with me?" The little boy was
shocked and ran away. Jade expressed dismay to her treatment
parent that she had tried to make friends with him. She found it
difficult to understand that her offer of sexual intimacy was not a
good way to make friends.

- History of brief relationships that end as soon as intimacy develops; and
- The use of sex to get nurturance and love.

Adversarial or manipulative behaviors—the abused child's
world has been a battleground where winning or losing means survival. Nothing is deserved, and nothing is freely given. She believes
that most transactions are based on sex, therefore, sex becomes a
source of power; prostitution is a logical extension. The child
becomes caught up in a vicious cycle of overwhelming neediness,
attempts to "force" others to meet her needs through various behavioral strategies, and finds herself even more empty as her demanding behaviors drive others away.

**Suicidal gestures or interpersonally motivated self-mutilation
(parasuicidality)**—extreme methods of controlling others. The child
uses these behaviors to force potentially important people to express
caring, validation, or appreciation. Self-mutilation, which can sometimes occur in the context of a strong therapeutic relationship, may
indicate the following:

- Therapy hurts,
- Therapy does not help the pain,
- Stop hurting me and be more loving, or
- I will hurt myself and make you feel like a bad therapist.

Hurting herself may also be the physical manifestation of psychic or emotional pain, which the child may use to overcome a feeling of numbness in the face of detachment or depersonalization.
Physical pain is easier to bear than emotional pain for the child.

Running away—Running away can sometimes occur when the
therapist is offering nurturance and parenting. This may be a therapeutic error on the part of the therapist, because these kinds of

relationships are too intense and intimate for the child. She has a problem with intimacy, as we have already seen, and mistrusts it as the beginning of a new cycle of abuse.

There can be no message like "I love you," for what is the response to that? "I love you too?" What has love always meant for this child? Instead, the effective therapist will offer emotional sanctuary, where every thought and expression is permitted and accepted. The therapist will be a guide, a reflection, and a sounding board.

Aggression—acceptance of a certain level of aggressiveness as "normal" in a relationship. The abusing adult has found aggression to be a good way of coercing others to comply with demands or for discharging rage and frustration. Aggression becomes a way of life. In turn, sexually abused children often externalize trauma through a high degree of verbal and physical aggression, destructiveness, and cruelty. Such behavior might lead to negative and rejecting responses from caregivers, which tend to increase the child's aggressiveness.

Avoidance—self-destructive activities used to "blank out" the pain. These may include drugs or alcohol; the ultimate avoidance is suicide.

Tension-reduction behaviors—behaviors that allow the child to take conflicts, issues, and tensions outside herself and externalize them (or act them out). These behaviors distract the child, act as a way of forestalling pain, and may include the following activities:
- Angry dramatics and acting out,
- Indiscriminate sexual activity,
- Substance abuse,
- Chronic overeating,
- Spending sprees,
- Risk-taking activities, and
- Self-mutilation.

The child develops patterns that can become repetitive and difficult to break and, as a result, she is sometimes seen as "addicted" to these tension reducers. Tension-reduction behaviors usually take the following pattern.
- The child experiences or anticipates the stressor.
- The stressor restimulates powerful feelings of rage, anxiety, helplessness, or self-loathing.

Karlie was 7 years old. Her caregivers suspected that she had experienced significant abuse, but Karlie had never been able to talk about it and had extreme difficulty controlling her emotions. Sometimes when she was upset she would rock back and forth on hands and knees and punch herself in the nose until she bled. It was only when she had reached this point that she seemed to find any relief from the constant anxiety that plagued her.

- The child is unable to regulate her own emotions (soothe herself) when unbearable psychic pressure (including a dread of pain) begins to build up.
- The child begins to search for a way to reduce the tension by selecting a strategy that temporarily distracts her, deadens the pain, restores self-control, fills perceived emptiness, soothes her, or relieves her from guilt or self-hatred.
- The child experiences a return of calm and relief but also guilt and self-disgust.
- The strategy or behavior is likely to be repeated because of the intense feelings of relief the child experiences.

Codependency—seeking out another dysfunctional person to respond to because the child has an underdeveloped sense of "self." The interaction with another dysfunctional person acts as a mirror and allows her to define herself using the other person as a reference point.

"Normal" Child Development

Development is an ongoing process that begins with conception and does not end until death. Each stage of a child's life involves physical, cognitive, social, and emotional development.

Physical development—growth of the child's body, including movement and muscle actions (motor development); development of smell, vision, hearing, taste, touch, and the ability to process information coming through the senses (sensory development).

Cognitive development—the development of the ability to think; to understand things in the child's world; to remember, reason, or to think things through; and the ability to form ideas and solve problems. The development of language (speaking and listening) is included in this area.

Zane came into care when he was 3 years old. His mother was a prostitute who had spent several weeks partying with her street friends. Someone finally called the child protection agency when one of the friends dangled Zane from the sixth-floor balcony by his ankles. During the previous weeks, he had been used as a sexual toy, taught to smoke "doobies," and to drink beer. He was a party favorite as he lurched, intoxicated, around the apartment.

He was a handful when he came into care. He made no eye contact and ran all the time. He did not listen to adults; in fact, he treated them as if they were not even present. He tore things apart, never slept, and seemed unable to focus on anything. A doctor finally gave the desperate foster mother Ritalin for him. That drug, however, made things much worse, so the foster mother took him off the medication. Finally the placement broke down, and Zane came to treatment foster care.

The clinical team conducted a developmental assessment and found him delayed on all levels. His language skills were nonexistent, self-help skills were primitive, and his ability to interact with others was significantly problematic. Even his gross motor skills were a problem, in that they were clumsy and often repeated over and over again. The team suspected a high-functioning form of autism and referred him to a local children's hospital for consultation.

While waiting for his turn at the clinic, Zane received sensitive care from his firm but understanding treatment parents. They offered numerous opportunities for stimulation, strong behavioral guidelines, and little by little they began to become a part of Zane's private world. By the time he reached the clinic, Zane was talking, maintaining eye contact, and learning some beginning social skills. The hospital team confirmed the problem; Zane's care had been so pathogenic that he had indeed developed many of the features of autism. He was, however, fundamentally "normal."

Social development—the development of the ability to have relationships, to learn how the world operates and the child's own role in the world, to determine how she will interact in the world, and to understand right and wrong.

Emotional development—the development of a sense of self that includes the child's personality, identity, the ability to give and receive caring, and expression of feelings.

Each of these developmental areas interact with each other, and one area of development will affect other areas of development. For instance, how would a child who is highly anxious (emotional development) learn to get along with other children (social development)? Would that child run, play, and get enough exercise (physical development)?

Any traumatic event (a shock or injury of some kind) will likely have developmental impacts, often in subtle, interacting ways. The charts in Appendix B describe "normal" development and how the trauma of sexual abuse might affect the child.

Recommended Reading

American Psychiatric Association. (1994). *Diagnostic and statistical manual of mental disorders* (4th ed.). Washington, DC: Author.

Bass, E., & Davis, L. (1988). *The courage to heal*. New York: Perennial Library.

Beeler, N. G., Rycus, J. S., & Hughes, R. C. (1990). *The effects of abuse and neglect on child development: A training curriculum.* Washington, DC: Child Welfare League of America.

Briere, J. N. (1992). *Child abuse trauma: Theory and treatment of the lasting effects*. Newbury Park, CA: Sage Publications.

Brohl, K. (1996). *Working with traumatized children: A handbook for healing*. Washington, DC: CWLA Press.

Cavanagh Johnson, G., Cavanagh Johnson, E., & Cavanagh Johnson, T. (1993). *Sexualized children: Assessment and treatment of sexualized children and children who molest*. Rockville, MD: Launch Press.

Macaskill, C. (1991). *Adopting or fostering a sexually abused child*. London: B.T. Batsford, Ltd.

Monahon, C. (1993). *Children and trauma: A parent's guide to helping children heal*. Toronto, Ontario: Maxwell Macmillan Canada.

Sgroi, S. (1982). *Handbook of clinical interventions in child sexual abuse*. Lexington, MA: Lexington Books.

2 Assessing the Impact of Sexual Abuse

Trauma Assessment Defined

When we first begin to work with a traumatized child, that child will be displaying the pain and aftereffects of abuse in a confusing array of symptoms. As a result, we have the challenging task of sorting through the symptoms to find a place to begin. A good first step is to ask the question, "Where and how does it hurt?"

With young and hurt children, we, as the caregiving adults, often feel a need to answer that question based on our own perceptions of the child's needs. It is much more difficult, but ultimately more useful, for the child to answer the question, if at all possible. This chapter offers a way of supporting a child as she examines her perceptions and the degree to which she has been affected, and as she identifies her own path to recovery.

What Is a Trauma Bond?

The victim of sexual abuse feels the impact of the abuse long after it has taken place. This ongoing connection to the trauma is known as a *trauma bond*.

There are a number of ways to understand the notion of being bonded to the trauma. One way relates to the victim's relationship with the abuser. If the child identified with or took on the role of protecting the abuser and so defines herself only in the context of this relationship, then she may be emotionally "bonded" with an individual who brutalizes or dehumanizes her. In this case, the child fantasizes that if she takes responsibility for the suffering, the suffering may eventually stop.

Another form of trauma bonding relates to the child's being caught up in a helpless cycle of negative ideas and thoughts, inability to meet goals, and misery about the abuse. Being "trapped in the misery" keeps the child psychologically and emotionally connected, or bonded, to the abusive events, whether she wishes it or not.

Finally, some children become bonded to the physical responses associated with the trauma. They either repeatedly set themselves up to reexperience the terror-based sensations surrounding the abuse or reenact the abuse in other relationships, this time in the safer role of aggressor. In either case, they use terror as a coping skill.

Becoming "disconnected" from the pain of the past requires that the child be given an opportunity to realistically explore the impacts of the abuse in an organized way. With support, the child can explore both positive and negative aspects of important relationships, discover what has been lost, understand how her own behavior has been shaped, and sort through where her development has been "trapped" because of the abuse. During the assessment process, the therapist can guide and support the child in her efforts.

What Is a Trauma Assessment?

A *trauma assessment* is the process that a therapist uses to understand the impact of sexual abuse on a child and the extent of damage. The therapist assesses the child's perceptions of damage from the past and the current impact of abuse, and then anticipates what damage or impact might occur in the future.

This assessment is based on the victim's perceptions, not the perceptions of the therapist, which may be surprisingly different from the child's. Finally, the therapist uses the trauma assessment to help the child understand that she has been affected by abuse and to identify what the child's treatment needs will be.

Purpose of the Trauma Assessment

Trauma assessment provides both the child and the therapist with a "road map" for treatment. The therapist's assessment will also help establish whether the child sees herself as a helpless victim of the abuse. (Research indicates that the more the child is able to see herself as a victim, the more likely she is to recover.) With an assessment, the therapist can look at what has happened in the past, how it is affecting the child in the present, and how it will impact her in the future.

An assessment is a structured way to assist the therapist and the child to process this information and to give the child solid indicators for her feelings, her sense of progress, and her understanding of the impact of the abuse. It provides a gauge for knowing whether or not the child is actually healing.

Assessment in a Psychotherapy Setting

Hindman has described a highly child-focused and sensitive trauma assessment process to use within the supportive environment of the psychotherapy setting. In this setting, the trauma assessment centers on exploration of the child's intimate thoughts, memories, and perceptions about important events and relationships around the abuse experience. The therapist acts as a guide, facilitator, and supportive ally as she leads the child assessment.

The therapist documents the results in a scrapbook, which will eventually contain the result of exercises the facilitator and child do together, important symbols, notes, drawings, or belongings that represent the work. The book can then be presented to a future therapist to use as a beginning point for treatment. It might also be shown to significant people in the child's life to help the child begin to communicate her thoughts and feelings about her experiences and then to begin a family healing process. This process can act as an important road map for recovery for children who are ready and able to make use of a therapeutic alliance.

Assessment in the Treatment Milieu

Some children, especially those who are so disturbed that they are placed in a residential treatment setting, are unable to form the kind of trusting relationship with an adult that is needed to make use of a traditional therapeutic relationship, such as that established in psychotherapy. These children, however, also desperately need to find a path away from the trauma bond.

A less informal approach to trauma assessment is often useful for these children. Based on a caregiver's ability to capture the "therapeutic moment" (an opportunity for teaching or exploration that presents itself in day-to-day living), the caregiver can help the child to explore ideas that will eventually lead to an understanding that something about the events of her past is acting as a script for her present.

The facilitator in this instance will be a caregiver, whose task it is to introduce the child to the notion that adults can be sensitive and understanding about the events of her past, that her behavior has meaning that she can understand, and that there is hope in allowing a therapeutic alliance to take place.

By using ideas and questions suggested by the trauma assessment tool, the caregiver can organize an effective approach to talking with the child. The caregiver can also use exercises and activities as the child is ready and able to engage in them. There may or may not be a "product" such as a scrapbook at the end, depending on the child's interest in exploring her issues in this way. When this more informal approach is successful, it can prepare and support the child to explore her issues more thoroughly later, perhaps in some other therapeutic format.

The Assessment Tool
Some Basic Notions

Those of us who work with children in care recognize the need for a way to conduct sensitive assessments of children who are resistant to the process of exploration. Our time frames are often far too short to conduct the thorough and supportive assessment that is completed in the therapist's office. We often need something timely and practical for use with children in out-of-home care.

The assessment "tool" we refer to here is an informal but structured process that will guide the conversations between a child and the therapeutic ally (therapist, caregiver, child welfare worker, group leader, etc.)

This tool identifies areas or dimensions where the child has been traumatized by sexual abuse and, within those areas, sets out questions to assess the degree and nature of the trauma. The caregiver will use these questions as guidelines to pursue "therapeutic conversations" with the child. The questions act as a springboard for discussing important issues in more depth as the child becomes more comfortable.

The questions are not meant to be used as a checklist. The caregiver or child protection worker should not pull up to the kitchen table with the child and proceed to ask the questions as if they were a survey to be filled in. We should resist any tendency to hurry through the questions and jump to a solution. As any individual experienced in working with difficult children already knows, being in a hurry will result in a child who is upset and highly resistant.

Instead, the questions communicate a set of ideas, thoughts for exploration, or places to look for understanding; they may be used as a framework for discussion when the appropriate therapeutic moment presents itself. The adult assessing the child asks questions in a musing, reflective style, as something for the child to think about. As the child responds, the adult clarifies, reflects, and sometimes confronts or points out inconsistencies.

Supportive exercises and activities are also effective tools to help the child along, as she becomes ready to use them. Exercises that emphasize *doing* rather than *talking* are often particularly welcome, as are activities that provide a child with fun, one-to-one time with a nurturing adult.

One particularly useful tool is the Feelings Scrapbook. This is a fun and helpful tool for children who do not have the basic vocabulary to discuss their feelings. The child and adult create a list of the feelings that people experience on a day-to-day basis. In discussion, the child will pick one feeling to focus on each day that she works on the book. She describes the feeling, assigns it a color, and together she and the adult use stories, drawings, or collages to explore the context in which such a feeling might occur or how it can be appropriately expressed. The images and colors that the child uses can then be brought into daily conversations as a reference point, when they are needed to explore some of the trauma assessment areas.

The reader is encouraged to explore some of the other resources listed at the end of this chapter for more ideas on therapeutic activities.

Caution: Not all children are ready to work on the issues of abuse in a direct way. Chapter 5 deals with managing children in a way that will help them to eventually reach the point where they can

Petra sat on the floor, curled into a tight ball. She cried as she rocked back and forth.

"I should never have let him touch me!" she sobbed. "If I had just said no, he would have gone away. I could have stopped it, and all of this would never have happened." Pat, her treatment parent, looked at her. "Petra, I'm confused. Didn't you just tell me you were four when he started?"

"Yes," Petra looked up.

"Let's think about that for a minute. Do you know anyone who is four?"

"Alice [Pat's granddaughter] is four."

"Right. So are you telling me that if your father tried to hurt Alice, it would be her job to stop him?"

"Don't be silly, Pat. She's just a little kid."

"I see. And little kids can't defend themselves against big grown-ups, can they? The grown-up has to stop himself with little children like Alice, don't they?"

"Yes, of course."

"So Petra, help me to understand. You think that when you were four, it was reasonable to expect yourself to stop the abuse, but anybody else who is four is just a little kid. Is that right?"

"I guess that's pretty stupid, isn't it."

"I don't think it's stupid at all, Petra. I think it's sad that you have been blaming yourself all along for something you never had control over. You were a victim, Petra."

---

focus on the abuse in the way described here. See Chapter 4 for a description of the stages of progress a child will need for this work.

An Image of Healing

If we were to think of a picture that represents the sexually abused child, her feelings, and her memories, we might make that picture a swirling circle of thick, black activity. The child is caught up in the swirl, unable to see clearly, unable to get out, unable to survive.

We might then picture the treatment process as the adult physically supporting the child to move up from the swirl, look down, learn about the swirl and understand it. With each new insight the child moves further away from the swirl, until finally she is far enough away that the swirl will not hurt her and she can see it for what it was, an event in the past which does not have to harm her today.

We view the trauma assessment tool as a pyramid, with each of the corners representing some aspect of the child's history. The child herself, as she gains distance and insight, stands at the top of the pyramid and looks downward. (See the figure on page 34.)

How does the adult help the child gain enough perspective so that she can see the events of her life "from the top of the pyramid," in a new way? By asking questions about the various parts of the pyramid and helping the child gain enough distance from the pain of the events to be able to analyze and draw self-healing conclusions. The pyramid then becomes a symbol for the child's own efforts to understand and heal herself.

Assessment versus Therapy

The assessment tool does pose some dilemmas. As the adult moves through the various dimensions of the child's life and discovers the self-blame and self-hatred that so often accompanies the aftermath of abuse, she will likely want to "solve" the problem. Not giving in to the temptation to take the pain away or solve the problem prematurely will help us avoid the trap of believing the validity of our own assumptions about what the child is feeling, and helps us focus and concentrate on the child's point of view.

Working through this structured assessment forces us to confront *all* of the impact of the abuse, understand *all* of the damage, and understand *all* of the treatment work to be done. Treatment that is based on a thorough trauma assessment will address all of the areas that support the child's hurt and process them away one at a time.

Assessment Dimensions

The adult will use the assessment tool to look at the events in the child's world from the child's own perspective. As the child attempts to consider the impact of and feelings about the abuse on the part of the offender and significant others, as well as her own ideas, she examines those ideas from three perspectives:

- **Relational**—both current and in the future, and how they are affected.
- **Developmental**—including physical and sexual development, cognitive development, and social and emotional development. Any or all of these areas may have been delayed or affected.

Victim's Viewpoint[2]

```
                    /\
                   /  \
                  /    \
                 /      \
                /        \
               /Traumatizing\
              / Event(s)     \
             /                \
            /_____\
```

Significant Others   Offender

- **Situational**—or memories of experiences surrounding the abuse that may be present. Colors, tastes, smells, seasons, etc., may have been paired with the details of the trauma and become part of the negative trauma experience. These ordinary life events, as a result, may now have become toxic to the child. This dimension also includes the child's general home environment.

Conducting the Trauma Assessment
Assessing the Impact on Relationships

There are three key areas of relationship that the child will need to explore to understand the effects of abuse on significant connections in her life. The *actual* relationships are not necessarily as important at this stage as understanding how the child *views* the relationships. These relationships include the child's relationship with the offender, the child's relationship with significant others in her life, and the child's view of the relationship between the offender and the significant others.

---

2. From J. Hindman, *Just before dawn* (Ontario, OR: AlexAndria Associates, 1989), pp. 252–253, with permission of author.

Relationship with the Offender

In this part of the assessment, the adult will follow a sequence of questions to support the child as she examines how she sees the offender, and how she believes the offender was seeing her at the time of the abuse. The child explores the context of that relationship, the roles, the importance of the relationship, and how those elements are connected to her view of how her identity has formed.

Questions around this dimension might include the following:

- What does the offender like about me?
- What does the offender not like about me?
- Why did the offender choose me?
- What did I like about the offender?
- What did I not like?
- What is the best and worst thing about this person?

Relationship with Significant Others

In this part of the assessment, the adult poses questions to help the child examine her relationship with the individuals she believes were in some way involved with or affected by the abuse. The child's first task is to list those people. This list might include siblings, the nonoffending parent, a teacher, or a member of the extended family.

Questions to ask about each of these individuals may include the following:

- How does the person see me? How do I see the person?
- What has been the impact of the abuse on the person?
- What has been the impact on me, in terms of this relationship?
- How do I feel about that impact?
- Does this person understand that I was a helpless victim? If so/ not, how do I feel about that?

Relationship Between Significant Others and the Offender

In this section of the assessment, the adult asks the child to again list each significant person in her life and then to examine the nature of the relationship between that person and the offender.

Questions in this area might include the following:

M arnie understood her relationship with her stepfather perfectly. He was a bored, ill, needy person who used her to feel like a man. Little by little she found herself turning into his "wife," caring for the children her mother and stepfather had together, making the household rules, and getting special little privileges.

Marnie watched her mother drift farther and farther away, becoming increasingly remote and uninvolved, eating and drinking and growing heavier and heavier. Her stepfather complained that she was no fun to be with anymore; Marnie made a much better partner.

It was not her stepfather who upset her. It was her mother. When Marnie disclosed the abuse, her mother refused to believe her. Marnie ended up leaving the home, losing her place, her job, and the people that needed her.

Meanwhile her mother took back her role as "wife and mother." Marnie struggled to understand why her mother had sided with her husband over her. She felt unloved, as if she did not belong anywhere, as if she was no one's child. Her struggle would be to build a future for herself apart from the parents who had betrayed her.

- How does that person view the offender? Does he/she believe that the offender did anything wrong? That the offender is a criminal?
- How does the offender view the significant person?
- What is the contact level between the significant person and the offender? Who initiates the contact?
- How does the significant person's relationship with the offender affect her relationship with the significant person and with the offender?

Assessing the Impact on the Child's Development

The developmental charts in Appendix B outline some of the typical developmental impacts of severe sexual abuse or trauma perpetrated on a child. Use these charts to locate the child developmentally and to determine where there are lags or problems that will need to be addressed.

This section discusses assessing the impact of sexual abuse on the child's growing sexual identity. The adult will examine the risks, strengths, impacts, and concerns about the child's sexual development. She will determine which areas need to change, and the victim's desire or ability to change in these areas, by using the following questions to evaluate three components of the child's sexual knowledge and development.

- Which of the following stages of sexual development and awareness was the child in at the time of the abuse?
    - **Unaware stage**. The child has a limited understanding of sex and about sexual abuse. If abused, the child would not have enough information to know that it was wrong. She may have cooperated, or even initiated, the abuse and enjoyed it as a form of closeness and contact.
    - **Unfortunate stage**. The child is becoming aware of sexuality and sexual issues and is beginning to understand what happened to her. She constantly criticizes and blames herself for her own gullibility. She experiences overwhelming feelings of self-disgust.
    - **Punishing puberty**. The child is aware of society's ideas about sexuality. She is uncomfortable with her own growing sexuality. Girls who begin menstruation are often deeply mortified, worried that they are damaged in some way, and convinced that they are bleeding to death.

      The idea that sexuality is secret and embarrassing is cemented when a child's parent is sexually uncomfortable. Boys who experience their first erotic dream may feel wrong and guilty but also feel confusing pleasure. These "normal" discomforts about sexuality open up a possibility for new trauma in the sexually abused child.
    - **Unresolved stage**. At this point, the sexually abused child has become an adult and is trapped in the trauma bond. Sexual development is arrested at the stage where the abuse originally took place. Normal, healthy intimate relationships are not possible.
- What information did the child have available at the time of the abuse about sexuality (normal and abnormal), and how did she view sexuality?

  Children who have been forced to build their sexual development on a history of sexual deviance have a much harder time recovering than children who have a sense of normal sexual relations. The adult will use the assessment to pinpoint areas where intervention, reeducation, and developmental repair work is necessary. To assess the child's level of sexual information, the therapist might ask the following questions.

- What values, morals, and religious influences about sexuality were available to the child?
- How much was normal sexuality talked about in the child's home? How acceptable was it to talk about sexuality?
- How much did the child know about the "mechanics" of sex (i.e., how the body works, what happens during sex, the pleasure associated with sex, sex in the context of loving relationships, etc.)?
- How much "street" information, including misinformation, did the child have at the time of the abuse?
- How much did the child know about the sexual relationship between her parents? What did she think went on between them? What was she told about this?
- How involved were the child's peers in sexual issues? Did she have any sexual experience with peers before the abuse?
- What had the child been taught about how women and men should act with one another?
- Had the child experienced sexual arousal yet? Did she have fantasies? Did she masturbate? Was she interested in the opposite sex?
- What are the "losses" or trauma associated with the abuse?

The abuse will have harmed the child's normal sexual identity. The adult may use the following questions to help explore where that harm lies in terms of how the child's sexuality has been affected:

- What interest or "appetite" does the child have for sexual activity? Is this developmentally "normal"?
- How does the child see her body? What part of her body image has been impacted by the trauma? What is the potential for the child to develop an eating disorder?
- Are there "body function problems" (elimination, digestion) that can be related to the abuse?
- Is the child able to communicate about her sexuality?

- Does the child have any sexual phobias, problems with sexual identity, or problems with unusual or absent arousal?
- How does the child use her sexuality? Is it a weapon, or does she use it to achieve some kind of intimacy or friendship?

Assessing the Situational Perspective

In this portion of the assessment, the adult examines the environment in which the abuse occurred. The purpose is to determine whether or not there is a risk for phobias to develop or whether there are cognitive distortions to be corrected. The adult may pose questions to examine details of the abuse, understand what senses were activated, and what cognitive connections may have been made.

Details of the abuse—What actually happened? What stage of the continuum of abuse was the perpetrator in? Where was the child touched, by what part of the perpetrator? What was the first incident like? The last one?

Activated senses—Which of the child's senses were activated (touch, smell, sight, sound, taste)?

Cognitive connections—What kind of cognitive (thinking) connections has the child made about the abuse? Questions leading to a better understanding about this might include the following:
- Where did the abuse happen?
- What was the physical environment like? How was it lit? What colors, temperature, etc., were involved?
- What happened in the 30 minutes prior to the abuse?
- How did the child feel about the offender during the abuse?
- Where were other people, and how did the child feel about that?
- What kinds of sexual conversations went on? What was talked about? What words were used?
- What were the tactics for coercion and enforcing compliance?
- What could the child see at the time of the abuse (not just the perpetrator, but the surroundings as well)?
- What was the child's own sexual response? How does she feel about that?
- What did the child feel in the 30 minutes following the abuse?
- What were the child's thoughts and fantasies about wanting to tell?

Daniel's mother and father, both of whom had abused him, won supervised access to their son in a court hearing. Daniel very much wanted these visits, too. Once-a-month visits began at the Children's Aid Society offices. Daniel's treatment parents noticed that, as time went on, he became more anxious around the visits, and after the visits, his behavior was outstandingly destructive. He urinated on the carpet in his room and tore off most of the wall board. The treatment team was deeply concerned. What was happening during the visits that could account for this increasing level of agitation?

"Nothing," the visit supervisor replied. "They are very pleasant visits. They sit and play cards most of the time."

The visit supervisor had not been informed that card playing had formed an important part of abuse in Daniel's family. The five children were forced to draw a card, which gave them the order in which they were to come in to their parents' bed. Until their turn came, they were to sit lined up on the carpet in their parents' room, watching and waiting.

Daniel reexperienced all of the anxiety, fear, rage, and dread during family visits as the card game began. When the card games were stopped, and when Daniel was told why they were stopped, the behavior ended.

Assessing the General Environment

There may have been aspects of the family's lifestyle that were important to the abuse situation and that led to further trauma. Some of the questions about the general surroundings might include the following:

- What was the family's level of affluence/poverty?
- What job/s did the caregivers have?
- What was the state of the physical and mental health of members of the family?
- What was the general level of family communication?
- What were the family structures, roles, power bases, decision-making patterns, control patterns? Was there a sense of connectedness to the community?

Chapter 7 offers more detail on this topic.

Putting the Assessment to Use

The process of trauma assessment will not "cure" the aftermath of abuse. Instead, it allows the adult and the child to examine, clarify, and unearth many of the memories and feelings surrounding the abuse in a structured and focused way. The trauma that the child had superficially kept under wraps with defense mechanisms and coping strategies can now "rear its ugly head."

The feelings that come with the trauma are "ugly" too. Therefore, the immediate effects of doing a trauma assessment will not always be positive. Talking and thinking about these memories may stir up powerful negative feelings. The child may feel angry, depressed, and in a state of upheaval.

Alternatively, younger children may not see the process as meaningful, because they are as yet unable to understand the nature of the trauma. In these cases, an assessment may be more valuable to the people surrounding the child than it is to the child.

Whether done formally or informally, the process offers two important things. First, it will provide both the adult and the child with a map for treatment. Choosing which road to take, including whether or not to try group work or psychotherapy, is one of the last pieces of the trauma assessment. Second, it will have made a contribution to the child's treatment because the act of sorting out feelings and memories is therapeutic in itself.

In the case of the formal assessment, as a final step the adult and the child need to make a decision about what will happen to the assessment (including any scrapbooks or products). They will need to make decisions about where to keep it, with whom it may be talked about, who to share it with, and what to do about it. The child needs to accept "ownership" for it as a "map" of her own reality.

At this stage, the assessment is one of the few events surrounding the abuse that the child can exert any control over, so what the child chooses to do with the assessment is extremely important. One choice might be to share the "product" of the assessment with a supportive and caring significant other, in order to talk about it and feel nurtured or cared for. Another option, especially important for children who have only dim and confused memories of the abuse, might be to stop the work. This is a decision that is possible if the child can feel good about it. And finally, yet another option might be to proceed to therapy, and try to work through some of the issues and difficulties that have been pointed out in the assessment process.

Recommended Readings

Burns, M. (1993). *Time in: A handbook for child and youth care professionals*. Toronto, Ontario: Burns-Johnston Publishing.

Crisci, G., Lay, M., & Lowenstein, L. (1997). *Paper dolls and paper airplanes: Therapeutic exercises for sexually traumatized children*. Charlotte, NC: Kidsrights.

Hindman, J. (1989). *Just before dawn*. Ontario, OR: AlexAndria Associates.

Hindman, J. (1991). *The mourning breaks: 101 "proactive" treatment strategies breaking the trauma bonds of sexual abuse*. Ontario, OR: AlexAndria Associates.

James, B. (1989). *Treating traumatized children: New insights and creative interventions*. Lexington, MA: Lexington Books.

3 Understanding Treatment for Abused Children

Treatment Defined

Treatment of a child who has been sexually abused is about helping her find a better way to survive. The child has been struggling to survive her fear, emptiness, and memories all along. She has found ways to cope as best she can. Some of the coping strategies have developed into such strengths as self-sufficiency, a sense of humor, being good in a crisis, or being a high achiever. Other ways of coping have become self-defeating and destructive (stealing, substance abuse, promiscuity, eating disorders). Whatever the chosen coping strategy, it deserves to be honored and celebrated for what it is—a way that helped the child survive in a toxic environment.

Treatment is not a cure, because the child is not sick. Instead it is a process of helping the child learn to distinguish between the healthy and the destructive aspects of her coping skills. With help, she can maximize her strengths while actively changing the patterns that are no longer useful or even destructive.

The task of the therapeutic adult is to create the *emotional sanctuary* the child needs to do the work of healing. This place will have the following characteristics:

- It will be safe (based on clear boundaries, rules for interaction, and an absence of exploitation).
- The people in this place will be respectful and celebrate the child for who she is—confusions, ambivalence, pain, rage, and all.
- The place and the people in it will give the child the power of setting her own treatment agenda (self-determination).
- The people in this place will concentrate on solving problems and not on why the problem exists (health-focused versus

pathology-focused) and allow the child to feel optimistic about the future.

The adult needs to understand that the child yearns for rescue, protection, and even love, and that the child will project whatever image she has of those things on to the adult. That image, however, is a "fantasy" that has always been disappointing in the past, because the child's wishes can never be met. Instead the knowledgeable adult will help the child understand that *this* relationship is for learning and growing. The adult is the guide/teacher in a "real" relationship that can be counted on and that forms the basis on which to do some hard work.

Who Can Provide Treatment?

The debate about who should and should not provide "treatment" to abused children has gone on almost since we have become aware of the abuse of children. Sometimes we believe that treatment is best left to the medical profession, other times we believe that treatment can best be done by nonmedical professionals in residential settings, by lay people, or even by survivors of abuse. The "invention" and growth of the treatment foster care model has added a new dimension to the debate, in that the model merges concepts from psychiatry and psychology with practical techniques from the residential treatment approach; those concepts and techniques are then "transplanted" by a clinical team (social work, psychiatry, psychology) into the dimension of corrective family living.

In this environment, we have learned, a well-trained and well-supported caregiver is capable of developing the responsive relationship and providing the emotional sanctuary that is necessary for a child to make real therapeutic progress. In these settings, other forms of treatment (group work, psychotherapy) are viewed as supplementary, not the sole form of treatment. The debate then shifts from "Who can treat?" to "What kind of treatment would be best for this child?" and "Which specific issues should each form of treatment address?"

In this chapter, we explain the goals and process of treatment in a general way, because they are common to all of the forms of treatment. (In the next chapter we will describe in more detail some of the various modes of treatment.) By reviewing the fundamental goals of treatment, the reader can anticipate how various treatment formats might interact with one another.

Foster caregivers, particularly, can see how their work in the day-to-day living environment might be considered a form of "treatment." Indeed, in some cases daily care may be the *only* treatment the child is ready for. When other forms of treatment are also in place, therapeutic daily care contributes to a total "treatment package." We encourage practitioners of the various treatment approaches to look at an expanded role for the child's caregiver* in their own clinical planning by considering ways that daily care can contribute to meeting therapeutic goals.

The Goals of Treatment

In general, the purpose of treatment is to assist the child to heal from the impact of sexual abuse. This is, however, a tall order. We find it more useful to look at goals that usually need to be met in the context of a therapeutic relationship. Broadly stated, the following are the goals of treatment for the aftermath of sexual abuse.

Goal 1—*Providing a safe release of feelings*, both positive and negative, around the abuse experience.

Goal 2—*Overcoming the symptoms and behaviors* that are currently disturbing the child's good functioning and making the appropriate connections between the behaviors and the abuse.

Goal 3—*Helping the child to understand* what part of her thinking has been affected by the abuse and helping her correct those distortions. (See *cognitive distortions*, page 15).

Goal 4—*Helping the child to overcome self-blame and self-hatred* and to replace them with self-respect and the ability to honor herself and her survival strategies.

---

*Note: In this chapter, the term "caregiver" refers to the person most directly involved in the child's treatment. In the therapeutic foster care environment, this would be the foster parent.

Goal 5—*Assisting the child to build a sense of trust* in herself and in a positive future.

Goal 6—*Enabling the child to gain a sense of perspective* about the abuse and to gain the *emotional distance* necessary to keep the trauma from hurting her in future.

Goal 7—*Supporting the child as she comes to terms* with her own sexuality, including good feelings surrounding sexual behaviors, masturbation, and the ability to discriminate healthy sexuality from the abuse.

Exploring the Goal Areas

Each of the preceding goal statements describes a dimension of the healing process. The child needs to explore, discover, and make decisions in each dimension. The following section addresses the issues that the child will face within each goal area. The caregiver will plan methods to help the child address these issues as a step in facilitating the child's work in each goal area. We have provided some questions and examples to help the caregiver plan the child's treatment.

Goal 1: Release of Feelings

As a victim of abuse, the child could not afford to feel the full extent of her emotions or to understand how hopelessly conflicted those emotions often were. She could not think about hating, telling on, and/or killing her abuser when she might also have relied on that person for food, shelter, or nurturing. She could not come to terms with the positive, even loving, feelings she felt for the abuser.

She therefore learned quickly not to trust her emotions or feelings. Her feelings had, in the past, led to betrayal, mistrust, violence, or destruction. She may have learned to block out pain, either because it was too devastating or because she did not want to give the abuser the "satisfaction of seeing me cry."

The following questions might act as good starting points for a therapeutic conversation. Within the safety of the therapeutic relationship, and with the help of an adult guide or "teacher for growth," the child may be able to use these questions to discover and explore her thoughts and feelings. A tool such as the Feelings Scrapbook (see page 31) might be a helpful way of focusing the discussion.

- Can the child recognize her feelings and tell them apart? Can the child feel a wide or limited range of emotions?
- Does the child have trouble expressing her feelings?
- Is the child afraid of her feelings? Do they seem out of control to her?
- Does the child value her feelings or just see them as self-indulgences or weaknesses?
- Is the child comfortable with anger, happiness, sadness?
- Does the child often feel confused?
- Is the child prone to depression, panic, nightmares?
- Has the child ever been violent or abusively angry?

Goal 2: Overcoming Symptoms and Behaviors

Coping is what a sexually abused child does to survive. However, not all of the ways of coping are positive. Coping mechanisms may have been "running away," either actively by leaving home or abusive situations, or passively through sleep, books, or fantasy. She may have turned to alcohol, drugs, or other addictive behaviors such as sex, eating, lying, stealing, or gambling to help mask the memory and/or the pain of the abuse.

She may have attempted to regain a sense of control by creating chaos, "spacing out," being hypervigilant, or keeping busy. For example, she may have become an overachiever or taken on the responsibility of caring for brothers and sisters at home. She may have forgotten what had happened to her, withdrawn into herself, or cut off her feelings. She may have minimized the abuse and pretended that it did not happen. She may have rationalized the abuse by creating excuses for the abuser, as well as for those who didn't believe her.

She may have developed a way of seeing people as being either all good or all bad. This allowed her to hold opposite, unintegrated points of view. For example, she may separate the father on whom she depends for love, support, and protection from the father that abuses her. The cost of preserving her image of the "good father" is that, in order to make sense of the abuse, she therefore views herself as the "bad daughter." Other, more disturbing, coping strategies might include mental illness, self-mutilation, or suicide.

Questions related to these symptoms will need to be addressed within a therapeutic relationship. Following are some examples:

- Has the child convinced herself that the abuse really was not so bad, since it did not kill her? Does she look for ways to let her abuser off the hook so she can avoid the pain of the full anger she has for the abuser?
- Is it safe for the child to remember? Does the child have a "psychological closet" into which she has shoved her memories? Can she recognize the behavioral "tricks" she uses to keep from remembering?
- Does she feel crazy with fury or depression one second, and then struggle to maintain a facade of cheeriness the next? Why does she think this happens?
- Is the need to be "perfect" strong? Did she try to use "perfect" behavior to avoid the abuse? What happens if she tries to let go now?
- Is the child tremendously consumed with the need for control? Does she feel like she will die if she does not get her own way? Why does she believe that?
- Do "crises" somehow follow her wherever she goes? Does she create crises to distract herself?
- Does she understand that some of her self-destructive behaviors are related to the abuse? Can the child honor the fact that she developed these behaviors to survive? Can she celebrate her own creativity, resiliency, and will power?
- Now that the child is in a safer environment and situation, can she understand that she has many resources and options? Can she choose to keep the behaviors that work for her and discard the self-destructive ones?

Goal 3: Overcoming Cognitive Distortions

When a child is abused, her perceptions become threatening to her. For example, it would be too overwhelming for her to admit that her father, who cared for her and took her to the park, had a frightening smile on his face while he was sexually abusing her.

If the significant adults in her life tell her that the abuse experiences did not really happen or that they happened differently than she perceived them, she will feel unsure, confused, and distressed about what is real. The incidents might be denied by a father who says that he was just tucking her in or by a mother saying that it was just a dream. She might be told by a teacher or minister that her father is a pillar of the community. The child may have an unusual understanding of the events and circumstances, or may have made illogical connections to try to make sense of the abuse. In this case, the child may constantly be confronted by a world that sees things differently from her own perceptions.

The child therefore may begin to think, "Am I really mistaken? What is real? Why does it feel so bad?" Living with such a dilemma makes it difficult for the child to trust her inner voice. She is afraid of what that voice might tell her and cannot trust the accuracy of what it says.

The therapeutic encounter that helps a child learn to trust her own thinking might include the following questions:

- How has the child tried to make sense of the abuse? What kinds of "thinking leaps" has she made to make sense of it?
- What life events have been "ruined" by this experience? How?
- How have her wishes, worries, and terrors changed her recollection of events?
- Does the child suffer from unpleasant, intrusive memories or reexperiences of the event (flashbacks)? Can she talk about those intrusions?
- Does the child have trouble listening to her intuitions? What does her inner voice tell her? Is it a good, reliable inner voice from the caregiver's point of view? Can the child be encouraged to trust it?
- Does the child misinterpret the behaviors and intentions of others? Is she chronically suspicious of the intent of others and always on guard? Can she be helped to interpret more realistically?
- Does the child lack the motivation to try new things? Does she believe that everything she tries will turn out badly? How can she be helped to overcome her self-doubts, take risks, and experience success?

Goal 4: Overcoming Self-Blame

A child will often believe that she is to blame for being sexually abused. The child may have been told explicitly by the abuser that it was her fault (e.g., "You're a bad girl. You really want this. You're so pretty that I couldn't help myself."). The child may have been punished when she did tell. She may have been accused of lying. The subject may never have been discussed again, giving the message that it was too terrible to talk about. Religious beliefs may convince the child that she is a sinner, unclean, or "damned to hell."

If the child were to allow herself to blame the abuser, she would be forced to realize that her world is an unsafe place where adults are untrustworthy and out of control and where she is vulnerable and powerless. Blaming herself can be a preferable solution to acknowledging such helplessness.

Therapists might ask the following questions to help the child process issues of self-blame. Helping her process these ideas may assist her in understanding the futility of blaming herself.

- Does the child feel bad, dirty, or ashamed?
- Does the child feel different from other people? Is she worried that there is something wrong deep inside her that would cause people to abandon her if they knew about it?
- Does the child have a hard time nurturing herself or receiving kindness?
- Does the child feel ashamed for needing attention and affection? Does she believe she can only get that kind of caring through sexual interactions?
- Does the child feel guilty for causing her own abuse? Does she believe that if only she had said "no," the abuse would have stopped? Does she believe that she was too attractive, that she put herself at too much risk, that her abuser could not help himself, or that deep down she must have wanted it?
- Does the child beat herself up emotionally for experiencing sexual or pleasurable feelings about the abuse?
- Does the child know that others do not view her nearly as harshly as she views herself?

Goal 5: Rebuilding Trust

Secrecy, isolation, and fear replace the trust, sharing, and confidence a child has about her safety when she is abused. The victim tends to see trust as an absolute and does not trust anyone at all or becomes so desperate for trust that she throws all her trust at the first likely target. Invariably she ends up feeling disappointed or abandoned, thus reinforcing her original beliefs—that people are not trustworthy and that she is not trustworthy.

The child will need to take huge risks to overcome the inability to trust. The following list of questions may help her articulate what she needs to "succeed" in trust relationships.

- Who will I pick to trust?
- How long should I know a person before I try to trust him or her?
- Do I have good communication with this person?
- What kind of thing will I trust the person with?
- How will I explain to this person what my behaviors mean and what is important to me?
- How will I make my expectations clear?
- How will I recognize if there are any elements of the relationship that parallel my abuse? How am I likely to react if there are?

Goal 6: Gaining Perspective

All of the "processing" (guided exploration) questions posed earlier in this chapter are structured to provide the child with the opportunity to gain some perspective about herself. As the child progresses, her perspective will change. The emotional roller coaster she experiences during the active treatment process will even out. She no longer doubts what happened to her, and begins to see that she is "more than her abuse." She affirms the strengths she has developed, and recognizes her own resiliency and the drive to be healthy. Finally, having faced her demons, she makes the changes she can and lets go of those things that are not in her power to change.

Goal 7: Supporting the Child

One of the biggest areas of impact of sexual abuse is the loss of a sense of self. The child sees herself only in terms of her abuse, and her abuse is who she is. Life is nothing but reaction to abuse.

A more positive, healthy identity needs to be created before the child can begin to process the aftermath of abuse. The child needs to have new life experiences, to have the opportunity to be acknowledged, and to reevaluate her experiences, decisions, and conclusions. Once a kinder, gentler "sense of self" is constructed, the other work on posttraumatic symptoms can begin.

This is the place to begin the treatment process.

4 Methods of Treatment

The therapist/caregiver can use a wide variety of resources and approaches to help a child overcome the aftermath of sexual abuse. Available resources might include the following:
- Individual psychotherapy,
- Family intervention (discussed in Chapter 7),
- Group therapy, and
- Residential therapeutic milieu.

Each of these approaches has its own strengths and drawbacks, and the child may need a combination of interventions. Any or all of these approaches together can form the treatment support the child needs to be able to heal. Selecting the form(s) of treatment will depend on the goals for the child, the match between the goal and the service being considered, and the child's preferences and likelihood of participating in and benefiting from the model being offered.

Individual Psychotherapy

Individual psychotherapy is a corrective and educational experience that teaches new attitudes and patterns of behavior to a child who is experiencing psychological difficulties. Psychotherapy is used as a time-limited intense experience, in conjunction with a safe and positive daily living experience, to help the child focus on particular goals, or when other forms of correcting the difficulty prove not to succeed. Individual psychotherapy may include the following components:
- A relationship between the child and a positive, friendly, and helpful person (the therapist);

- A safe environment;
- Reliable and sensitive responses from the adult to the child; and
- Support for the child.

There are many different types of psychotherapy, each with its own supporting theory. Therapists themselves do not necessarily agree on how therapy should proceed, or what areas they should delve into. All forms of therapy, however, begin with a thorough assessment and an attempt to select a beginning point and techniques that are appropriate to the child.

Individual psychotherapy serves a specific purpose in the overall treatment plan, as discussed in the following section. It is perhaps most useful when the child's case management team is clear on where it wants to go and can ask the psychotherapist to complete certain specific tasks.

The Purpose of Individual Psychotherapy

To those outside of the process, psychotherapy can seem like a mysterious "black box." Sometimes the only clue for what might be going on in therapy is the child's troubling and explosive behaviors before and after sessions. It is therefore understandable that caregivers are suspicious of the value of psychotherapy. Research results suggest, however, that an absence of good communication and partnership between therapist and caregiver when the child is in psychotherapy actually blocks the child's progress in both settings.

Children placed in treatment foster care or residential treatment settings pose special demands for such partnerships. In these 24-hour treatment settings, caregivers follow up active assessment and treatment planning with planned intervention. It would be foolish to think that something is going on once a week for one hour that will be more "therapeutically important" than what happens in the rest of the child's week. It would be equally foolish, however, not to appreciate and maximize the opportunity a child has of experiencing a separate, focussed relationship outside of the daily living environment.

We have found that the key to a successful partnership lies in understanding the relative value of each form of helping and ensuring that good communication occurs between members of the child's treatment team.

Broadly, psychotherapy is a process in which the child/therapist relationship is used to support the child through the treatment tasks discussed in Chapter 3. There may be differing approaches or techniques, depending on the therapist, but in general the therapy setting allows the child to express and explore feelings in a safe way when she is usually not able to express them in other settings.

Sometimes expressing strong feelings in the sessions carries over into the daily care environment, either in the form of overexcitement, anxiety, or other strong feelings. The therapist must be aware of the child's ability to tolerate the process or regulate her emotions and carefully plan and adjust sessions accordingly. It is rarely, if ever, helpful to have the child's daily living environment disrupted by the emergence of strong feelings to the point where a placement is jeopardized.

When individual therapy is working well, however, it can play an important part in a child's recovery process. For instance, in cases where children feel torn by loyalty binds between the caregiver and the biological family, a therapist can help sort through those feelings. Some children prefer to "protect" the relationship with the caregiver by holding back their experiences; therapy is helpful in assisting the child to come to better terms with her experience of victimization. When some aspect of the relationship with the caregiver begins to mirror or trigger an abuse experience, the safety and privacy of the therapist's office provides an important opportunity to explore how the past is writing the script for the experiences of the present. When the therapist is skilled, children can receive expert guidance in exploration of important events and feelings; this can accelerate the healing process. Listed below are some of the specific purposes of psychotherapy:

- To provide another avenue in which the child can grow and change;
- To address specific concerns that arise in other areas of the child's life;
- To prepare the child for the benefits of a group experience by offering an opportunity to explore the impacts of abuse in a more contained, less public way first; and
- To provide support in whatever way the child finds helpful.

Common Misperceptions about Psychotherapy

Children who have been abused, especially those in residential or foster care, often show such high levels of emotional and behavioral disturbance that their case managing social workers refer them to psychotherapists for treatment. The results can be disappointing, however. Those disappointments arise out of some common mistaken ideas about the limitations of the therapy process, as listed below.

- **The child is referred for the wrong reasons.** Caregivers sometimes make mistaken referrals to psychotherapy, because they have misunderstood the source of the distress. For instance, if the child has had multiple placements, is in a state of "limbo" (where the child's future living place is largely unknown to her), or is actively grieving a difficult separation, the answer is not psychotherapy, but good case management.

- **The child's day-to-day living situation is unsupportive.** If the child's caregivers are punitive, not supportive, or are using management techniques that are maintaining the child in a constant state of feeling unsafe, then psychotherapy will not address these issues. A more helpful response would be to stabilize the living environment and help caregivers be more responsive to the child.

- **The behavior does not improve.** The child will not necessarily behave better as a result of psychotherapy. Indeed, she may begin to behave badly as her personal defenses, which have helped her to survive up to this point, are challenged. If the behavioral fallout from psychotherapy cannot be managed in the daily environment, then active steps must be taken to stabilize and support the day-to-day care situation. Stability of living situation and security in primary relationships will *always* need to take precedence over psychotherapy.

- **Psychotherapy takes a long time and requires a planning commitment.** The damage endured by the child can be extreme, especially when the abuse took place in the context of severe neglect, family chaos, attachment difficulties, and disruption. Not every psychotherapist is able to remain involved with a child in the face of stubborn resistance, and long-term psychotherapy is expensive. For the child who has difficulty trusting and building relationships in the first instance, beginning a course of psychotherapy that will not be completed may do more harm than good.

Psychotherapy can be a helpful and important part of a well-thought-out intervention plan, but it cannot take the place of good case management, appropriate and stable care, and thoughtful daily management.

Criteria for Referring a Child to Psychotherapy

Psychotherapy cannot meet all expectations. Treatment need is different from treatment readiness, as we shall see, so it is important to be realistic when considering this form of intervention.

For the child to make use of individual psychotherapy, the following criteria need to be in place prior to referral.

- The child exhibits treatment readiness as well as treatment needs. Readiness will appear in the following way:
  - The child has shown evidence of being able to form at least one good relationship and was able to maintain it even in the face of frustration or conflict.
  - The child does not respond to inner conflict or tension by immediately acting it out. By its very nature psychotherapy produces tensions. If the child cannot allow herself to work these tensions out inside herself rather than through behaviors, she is not a good candidate for the traditional form of therapy.
  - The child can remember and talk about (or play about, in the case of play therapy) some of her major conflict areas. The child who is afraid of her own feelings or worried about how others will react to those feelings will find the emotions stirred up by psychotherapy to be threatening to her security.
- The child has some understanding that the psychotherapy will focus on changing her own contribution to her problems or help her to learn to cope with them differently. Psychotherapy cannot change the things beyond the child's control (i.e., who her family is, her placement dilemmas, or clarity about her future).
- The child has ongoing support provided by a primary caregiving figure, and that caregiving person has developed a working part-

nership with the therapist. The child has a sense of day-to-day safety that protects her against future victimization.

- Psychotherapy for the child will be operating at the same time as other interventions that will address the need for change in the family or other important areas of the child's life.

- The therapist is skillful, goal oriented, and clear in her thinking about how treatment will work. She demonstrates good judgment, competency, sensitivity to the issues, and the ability to function appropriately as a part of the helper system. She is prepared to communicate regularly and fully to other members of the child's treatment team.

- The case managing agency is strongly committed to supporting the therapeutic process once therapy begins. Such support includes active communication, inclusive decision making, continuity in decision making when there are personnel changes, and financial resources that remain available. Case managers need to be sensitive to the issues involved in treating the aftermath of sexual abuse and be well-informed advocates for their young charges.

Types of Individual Treatment

Individual psychotherapy for children can take many forms: play therapy, cognitive/behavioral therapy, expressive therapies, and psychopharmacology. We have provided brief descriptions of each form to aid the case manager and/or caregiver to determine the appropriate method of treatment.

- **Play therapy** is treatment that works with and through the child's play. This is best for children ages 2 to 11, where play is naturally employed for problem solving. If the child can communicate her experiences symbolically (by pretending or working through issues on experiential terms) and to some degree verbally, she may be a candidate for play therapy.

- **Cognitive/behavioral therapy** focuses directly on changing the child's maladaptive behaviors and the mistaken thoughts that fuel those behaviors. The therapist sets specific goals and develops activities, games, and role plays that provide the child with an opportunity to think about problems in new ways and to develop a new set of beliefs or behaviors that are more helpful.

- **Expressive therapies** use art, music, and movement to help children explore their trauma and begin to heal. Many memories that children have are not attached to words but are instead related to body sensations, sight, or sound. Expressive therapies are particularly helpful in these situations and help children reach into their memories without the use of words. The child can explore and express the feelings that she cannot express in "talking" therapies. Used in conjunction with other forms of therapy, expressive therapies widen the range of methods available to the child to communicate.

- **Medication (psychopharmacology)** can be used to relieve symptoms in conjunction with other therapies. Anxiety, depression, or sleeplessness often follow trauma. These symptoms can become so intense that medication is needed for relief. Medication, however, is not a substitute for other forms of therapy. The decision to medicate a child cannot be taken lightly; medications may have side effects or lead to dependency and future abuse of the drug. Another concern is the emotional side effect of moving self-control to something external (i.e., a pill). Used appropriately, medication can be useful in helping a child feel less anxious or distressed so she can generally function more satisfactorily. This kind of general improvement will also facilitate better use of other forms of therapy.

Group Therapy

Group therapy is often described in the literature as the "preferred" form of treatment for children, because it allows children to confront and work through their experiences with a group of peers who are struggling with the same issues. However, as with psychotherapy, there is often a good degree of suspicion about the value of group work by foster parents, who see "worked up" children returning to their homes. The sessions themselves hide behind a shroud of mystery called "confidentiality," so the caregiver has little information about the child's experience. Under the worst circumstances, the foster caregiver cannot really support the child's attendance, feeling it does more harm than good.

Research has shown that, when this kind of lack of information and absence of caregiver support for the child to attend group occurs, the full value of either the group or the foster care experience is never realized. On the other hand, children who are well-supported in a sensitive care setting can make excellent progress when the lessons of the group experience are reinforced in their daily lives. It is therefore important for caregivers to have information about what happens to their children in the group setting and to understand the value of that experience. In this section we will look at the purpose and goals of group therapy and an example of how a group experience may be structured.

Group therapy involves gathering together groups of children who have been affected by a similar problem—in this case sexual abuse. The children are usually at a similar level of development but can come from any number of living circumstances (still at home to living in residential treatment or foster care).

While the specific content and number of group sessions can vary depending on the model being used, generally groups follow the same overall "pattern" of operating. There will be some form of intake interview, or assessment, to determine what level of crisis the child is in following the initial disclosure, how much support the child received around the initial crisis phase, whether the child has developed some individual strengths and coping abilities, and the child's readiness for a group experience.

After the initial assessment is completed, there will be some form of "contracting" with the child. The therapist will explain the "rules" of the group, share some sense of the experience, and help the child set personal goals to work on during the course of the group.

Each group session will have a similar structure. The group begins with the children's arrival, and a snack is served. (Food is incredibly important in groups, as it is an acceptable form of receiving nurturance.) The group leader lays out the content for the day's session. This is followed by a series of activities designed to help the children explore the topic and their feelings about themselves. The children have the opportunity not only to explore their own points of view, but to hear the views of others in the group as well. Finally, the children are given some homework or an activity that they are to practice during the week as a follow-up to what they learned.

Opportunities in Group Therapy

The group experience is a powerful opportunity for the child to explore her own reaction to her experiences, gain a better understanding of how her responses and behaviors are associated with the abuse experience, and to make choices that will eventually lead to healing. Groups are particularly helpful in this process, because the child will be exposed to others who have had experiences similar to her own. She will learn that she is not alone in her experience, as she may have felt. She will learn that some of her reactions and feelings are "normal" under the circumstances and that realization can alleviate some of her anxieties and fears about her functioning. Finally, she can work on these issues in an atmosphere of fun and good humor. Being able to reduce the problem to more human dimensions can be an important step in finally being able to feel powerful enough to grapple with it.

Listed below are some possible specific goals of the group experience:

- To have a positive counseling experience;
- To learn ways to express feelings honestly, directly, and safely;
- To be aware of differences and similarities between other families and the child's own family;
- To improve self-esteem;
- To understand how abuse in the home has affected her;
- To become familiar with the different types of abuse (i.e., physical, verbal, emotional, and sexual);
- To develop a working knowledge of the cycle of violence;
- To learn that the child is not responsible for the abuse in her home, nor could she have stopped it from happening;
- To develop a personal protection plan against abuse;
- To learn a nonviolent problem-solving approach;
- To explore personal losses and how they have affected her; and
- To share what she is learning in the group with significant others.

A Typical Group Structure

We have provided an outline[3] for a 17-week psychoeducational group experience for girls 9 to 12 years old. While the format and time allowances may vary, the outline highlights topics that children will typically discuss in a therapeutic group:

Session 1:	Getting to Know You
Session 2:	Self-Esteem Activity
Session 3:	Feeling Activity
Session 4:	Feelings
Session 5:	Families
Session 6:	Abuse
Session 7:	Personal Protection Plans
Session 8:	Anger
Session 9:	Personal Power and Assertiveness
Session 10:	Sexual Abuse
Session 11:	Grief, Separation, and Divorce
Session 12:	Choices
Session 13:	Revenge versus Self-Defense
Session 14:	Drug Abuse
Session 15:	Building Support Systems
Session 16:	Saying Good-bye to Group
Session 17:	Party

The Power of Groups

The child often feels singled out by the trauma of sexual abuse and concludes that something is therefore wrong with her. She feels lonely in her victimization. That loneliness can be lessened by sharing the experience with similarly traumatized peers.

A child is often stunned when she realizes that other children have had similar experiences. This discovery can free a child to speak up about her own experiences in an environment that she and her peers view as safe for them.

Since any group of children tends to gravitate toward fun, the experience of finding enjoyment together can often undo some of the terror and helplessness the child feels about the abuse. Together

3.   From M. Montgomery, *Children's domestic abuse program* (Charlotte: NC: Kidsrights, 1991) with permission of author.

the group members discover that they can be bright, have fun, and feel happy, even though the topic they have gathered together to discuss is one that has carried such shame and secrecy. The experience can provide a huge sense of relief as the child discovers she is much, much more than her abuse.

Groups provide children with the opportunity to express themselves through a number of different venues. Children can play roles in scenarios where they experience feeling empowered and capable of creating positive solutions to problems. Through play, art, and conversations the children are provided opportunities for exploration.

A shy child may be empowered to share or express hidden emotions through peer example. A child who has been unable to express a particularly painful memory may hear another, similar experience voiced through a peer's account, thereby reducing the terror and hold over her that the experience has held. Adolescent groups can be particularly helpful since teens most often look to their peers as their major source of support. As a means for helping the child gain some perspective, group therapy is among the most powerful of the treatment options.

Criteria for Referring a Child to Group Therapy

Just as in psychotherapy, a child can be in need of a group experience, yet not be ready to make use of one. Following are "group readiness" indicators to look for when making the decision about referring a child to group therapy.

- The child is able to make use of a treatment relationship, as evidenced by her ability to form and maintain at least one good relationship, even in the face of frustration and conflict.
- The child does not respond to inner conflict or tension by immediately acting it out. Children who are symptom ridden to the point where stress is likely to provoke severely avoidant behaviors such as self-destructiveness, dissociative episodes, or extreme regression; or severely aggressive behaviors such as assault or dangerous passive aggression, are not ready for groups.
- The child demonstrates some ability to talk about the abuse.
- The child is motivated to attend the group and has some sense that the group process will focus on changing her own contribu-

tion to her problems or help her to learn to cope with them differently. The child understands that the group experience cannot change things beyond the child's control (i.e., who her family is, her placement dilemmas, or clarity about her future).

- The child has an appropriate level of cognitive development for the group under consideration. Caregivers must consider such factors as maturation level, literacy, social skills, verbalization and thinking skills, and life stage in relation to the other children in the group.
- The child must be able to maintain the confidentiality of other group members.
- The child must have moved past the stage of coping with the events immediately after disclosure and be ready to examine the impact of the abuse experience on her development and functioning. A "crisis of disclosure" group or counseling opportunity may be required before a therapy group is considered.

The child's case management team must also demonstrate the following characteristics for the group experience to be a viable option:

- The person caring for the child is supportive of the child's attendance and has developed a working partnership with the group therapist(s). The caregiver is prepared and able to deal with any behavioral fallout that might occur as a result of the group experience, and the child has a sense of day-to-day safety that protects her against future victimization.
- The group therapist is skillful, goal-oriented, and clear in her thinking about how treatment will work. She demonstrates good judgement, competency, sensitivity to the issues, and the ability to function appropriately as part of the helper system. She is prepared to communicate regularly and fully to other members of the treatment team.
- The case managing agency is strongly committed to supporting the therapeutic process once group therapy begins. Such support includes active communication, inclusive decision making, continuity of planning, and good management of instrumental issues (i.e., a safe and consistent method of transporting to child to and from the group).

Debriefing After Group Therapy

Foster caregivers often complain that children return from their group experiences agitated, even seeming to be sexually aroused. This is certainly one of the possibilities when we gather together groups of children who have experience sexual abuse. This problem can usually be managed by providing the child with some quiet time with an adult and a chance to talk about the feelings that have been aroused by group discussion.

If the problem is recurrent, it should be discussed with the group leader. Care can then be taken to ensure that the group has a chance to debrief before it finishes a session.

Finally, care should be taken to have transportation after group available promptly. Often the problem is created in the unstructured time after group and before rides arrive, when the children are together with much less supervision.

If you have taken all precautions , and the child is still becoming aroused and reactive to the group experience, you might reconsider whether the child is ready for group. Perhaps more milieu-based work is needed first.

Residential Therapeutic Milieu

The *therapeutic milieu* is an out-of-home care environment for troubled and troubling children and youths where treatment is incorporated in the day-to-day care of the child. Ordinary living experiences become vehicles for planned change (treatment) when the caregiver or therapist uses them as opportunities for teaching new ideas, highlighting new experiences, and supporting new behaviors. Staff (child and youth workers, social workers, counsellors, nurses, etc.) are specially trained to use daily living experiences to support the development of the children who live within the therapeutic environment.

Certain features distinguish the therapeutic milieu and serve to highlight its potential for abused children. Predictability in routines, events, caregivers, and caregiving approach is typical. Safety and the absence of harm are another key feature. Behavior management techniques in the milieu are fair, consistent, planned and nonpunitive.

The most effective therapeutic living environments emphasize positive teaching.

The therapeutic milieu can help children to make new connections and insights, understand issues in a different way, and change their dysfunctional behaviors. The essential component in achieving this level of change is the presence of a sensitive caregiver capable of extracting "life lessons" from the events in the daily environment. "Capturing the therapeutic moment" is one way to describe how these adults are able to guide children to think things through and draw new conclusions. "Life space counseling" is another term that describes this supportive, corrective, teaching technique. The individual who employs these techniques is referred to as the "milieu-based therapist" or "therapeutic caregiver."

There are many examples of treatment milieus. Traditionally they involved staff-operated, group care living environments, such as group homes, residential mental health programs, rehabilitation centers, and even inpatient hospital wards for disturbed youths. These settings all use daily life experiences in a planned and corrective way to meet treatment goals.

Treatment Foster Care as a Therapeutic Milieu

Treatment foster care (TFC) is a relatively recent model that offers an excellent opportunity for milieu-based therapy. The family setting has been the main method of child rearing since the beginning of history and has proven itself to be effective in providing children with opportunities to develop the emotional attachments that they need to successfully learn social values and pro-social behaviors. Predictability, safety, consistency, and sensitive adult responses are as important in a foster care setting as they are in group care.

There are some advantages of TFC over the group care setting which lend themselves well to development of a therapeutic milieu. First, the caregiver-to-child ratio is likely to be very low, usually no more than two children per treatment home, so there is a comparatively high level of direct adult/child interaction. (We believe that high adult/child interaction may ultimately be found to be the key factor in why outcomes in the TFC setting are as promising as they are.)

Contagion, or the effect of sharing negative attitudes or behaviors between residents, is much less a factor in the family-based setting. There are fewer children, and they tend to be surrounded more by functional peers and adults than by a negative peer culture.

The treatment foster home is community-based and highly interdependent with the people and services of neighborhood, religious organization, and extended family. This allows children to experience a host of positive relationships in the surrounding community (school, religion, recreation) that can offer or reinforce learning opportunities while still being able to access the clinical support and structure of the treatment milieu.

Against this backdrop, treatment foster caregivers trained in the techniques of milieu-based therapy can develop a powerful therapeutic environment. TFC training typically addresses the following:

- Normal and abnormal child development,
- Counseling skills, and
- The needs of abused and traumatized children.

Such training allows caregivers to respond to children's needs in a highly sensitive, therapeutic manner.

Finally, treatment foster caregivers receive the clinical support necessary to gain perspective about each child, to assess the child's needs realistically, and to plan for ways to meet those needs. With the help of the rest of the treatment team, the treatment foster parent is able much more of the time to respond "from the head," and not just "from the heart." This encourages a "therapeutic distance" that, in our experience, allows a troubled child to do some in-depth work in a family-based environment.

Foster Care as a Therapeutic Milieu

A high percentage of children who make their way into foster care will have experienced sexual abuse in the past. While their needs may not be as acute as those referred to TFC, the children who are struggling in foster care to overcome the effects of trauma also require sensitive, responsive care.

The best of foster caregivers naturally have the special ability to be attuned to and aware of the messages of a child's behavior. These

Mr. and Mrs. Smith were talking about what color to paint the house. It was a lively discussion, full of laughter and good-natured ribbing, but obviously the final decision was going to require compromise. As they began to narrow the choices down, Mrs. Smith noticed Tommy looking at them oddly.

"Is something on your mind?" she asked.

"Why does he let you decide?" asked Tommy.

Mrs. Smith sat back and contemplated before she spoke. "Who should decide, Tommy?"

"Mr. Smith. He's the man."

"Because Mr. Smith is the man, he should be the one who makes decisions for us?"

"Yeah."

"Have you ever seen things work another way before? Where women make decisions too?"

"Well yeah, at school but that's different."

"Women at school are different than women at home."

"That's right, at home men are the rulers."

"So when men are the rulers, what are they allowed to do?"

"Oh, they can make people do what they want. You know, do stuff for them."

"Even if they don't want to?"

"Well I guess so, yeah."

"How do the women and children feel about being ruled?"

---

individuals have mastered the art of supporting children and "capturing the therapeutic moment." Often, however, foster parents complain that, while training provides them with a good sense of what to look for and what abuse is, they are much less confident about "what to do." These caregivers do not recognize the techniques of the therapeutic milieu (which they are so naturally good at) as a legitimate form of helping, and therefore do not view the techniques as "doing the right thing."

When provided with training and sensitization to the child's process of healing and a greater awareness of what can be done to support healing, foster parents can also offer a highly supportive and therapeutic living environment. Indeed, in the best of these settings, the care the child receives is all but indistinguishable from the more formal therapeutic milieu.

"Oh, they get mad. They don't like to be bossed around."

"So they don't like it, but the man makes them do what he wants. Do you think that's fair?"

"I guess not, but that's just the rules."

"Hmm, that's the rules. You believe that's the rules. How did you get the idea that was the rule?"

"Oh, from my stepdad and my mom. He made the decisions."

"Even if other people disagreed or felt bad? Do you think maybe that was the rule he made up because he wanted it that way?"

"What do you mean?"

"Well, not all families believe that is the right rule. Lots of families believe everybody should have a say, that everybody's opinion is important, men, women, children, everybody."

Mr. Smith piped in, "That's right, Tommy. I don't believe men get to rule. That is a kind of selfish way to think. It makes it seem as if other people are not important too, and they are. I might be the biggest and strongest here, but I'm not the most important. You are as important as I am. How you feel about things matters to me."

"Oh. Can I have a cookie?"

Mrs. Smith replied "Yes, one. Dinner is in an hour. Now about that misty lilac ..."

The Abused Child in the Therapeutic Milieu

For the child who has grown up in an abusive household, a trained caregiver in a therapeutic milieu can offer thoughtful care in a safe place to heal and grow. The therapeutic milieu can be a powerful resource in the healing process of the sexually abused child, because the emphasis on safety and predictability that occurs in a milieu maximizes the child's opportunity to feel free enough to begin to work. The caregiver in the therapeutic milieu is able to maintain the objectivity and therapeutic distance necessary to facilitate the child's attempts to explore.

Treatment team members can address the child's various growth needs in a number of different ways: through formal counseling sessions within the milieu; life space counseling sessions; skills training sessions (life skills, social skills, etc.); or by seizing the therapeutic moment as it occurs in adult/child interactions and turning it into a teaching opportunity. Caregivers can model effective relationships in the milieu, and the child can then experience them in a safe, nonthreatening way. Caregivers can observe, first hand, appropriate communication, coping strategies, assertiveness, and gender relationships. The child may have the opportunity to watch trusting relationships unfold and can participate in conversations about how that happens.

If the therapeutic milieu is family based, the child has a rich opportunity for observing and participating in a nonabusive family setting where relationships are not based on the commodity of sexuality. Instead, these relationships are based on mutual respect and true affection, providing the child with new ways of thinking about family relationships and thus changing the pervasive, multigenerational cycle of abuse.

The Importance of Communication with the Team

As we have seen, treatment takes on many forms. It does not only happen in groups, and it can happen in the daily living environment as well. In order for all treatment offered to be maximized, the members of the child's supportive team will need to communicate frequently and fully, because so many aspects of the child's existence will have therapeutic meaning.

The issue of open communication between members of the child's case management team sometimes causes concern for group and individual therapists. The concern relates to the sense that breaching the child's confidential disclosures by telling other members of the team without the child's permission will be just another intrusion to the child.

On the other hand, the child's caregiver is living with aspects of the child's story through her behavior on a daily basis and is struggling to understand what the behavior means. Sometimes caregivers avoid telling therapists some aspects of the child's daily experience, because it seems like a betrayal of the child.

Through a lack of regular and thorough communication, the child can become viewed in "sections" based on the contact the adult is having: the child in group, the child at home, the child in therapy. The caregiver may miss a sense of the child's total experience, because the information necessary to understand it has not been transmitted. This oversight does not allow the caregiving team to be aware of or offer the appropriate kind of support at clinically important times, such as the following:

- The child is beginning to try to put to use in one setting an insight achieved in another setting.
- An event in day-to-day living acts as a trigger to abuse memories.
- The daily behavior gives hints to issues that have been stirred up in the therapy session, but that the child is unable to talk about in a forthright way.
- The meaning of puzzling or troubling behavior has been made clear to one member of the team but not to another.
- The child begins to feel multiple loyalties toward the various helpers and either feels bombarded by input or afraid to tell one helper important issues for fear of hurting the feelings of another. This experience can act as a mirror of the earlier, dysfunctional family relationship patterns.

The danger of fragmenting our view of the child in this way is that we will inadvertently create an impression that, to us, the child is less important than her story of abuse and that she is nothing more than her abuse.

To the child, the interest her helpers seem to have in the abuse affects her own view of it as "important enough to hold on to." This view can actually become an impediment to progress. By paying attention to the whole child, on the other hand, and communicating about the child in a holistic way, the team can support and accelerate the child's growth in all of the therapeutic settings.

Additionally, when the helpers view themselves as costakeholders in a healing process, each can contribute her individual expertise and talent uniquely, rather than feel burdened with the demand to resolve the issues alone. This adds a level of interdependence and mutual accountability that actually improves service significantly.

It is important, therefore, for a contract for service between members of the child's helping team to include a requirement to communicate regularly on several issues:

- Daily progress,
- Significant life events,
- Behavioral changes and their context,
- New challenges, and / or
- Breakthroughs in thinking or processing.

Such communication is often best facilitated in a case conference scheduled no less than quarterly and as often as monthly when active issues are emerging. This level of sharing allows the development of a community of caring that is capable of celebrating a child's gains in a "public" way.

Recommended Reading

Bass, E., & Davis, L. (1988). *The courage to heal.* New York: Perennial Library.

Beeler, N.G., R ycus, J.S., & Hughes, R.C. (1990). *The effects of abuse and neglect on child development: A training curriculum.* Washington, DC: Child Welfare League of America.

Briere, J.N. (1992). *Child abuse trauma: Theory and treatment of the lasting effects.* Newbury Park, CA: Sage Publications.

Brohl, K. (1996). *Working with traumatized children: A handbook for healing.* Washington, DC: CWLA Press.

Burns, M. (1993). *Time in: A handbook for child and youth care professionals.* Toronto, Ontario: Burns-Johnston Publishing.

Crisci, G., Lay, M., & Lowenstein, L. (1997). *Paper dolls and paper airplanes: Therapeutic exercises for sexually traumatized children.* Charlotte, NC: Kidsrights.

Davis, N. (1990). *Once upon a time: Therapeutic stories to heal abused children.* Oxon Hill, MD: Psychological Associates of Oxon Hill.

DeLuca, R., Boyes, D., Furer, P., Grayston, A., & Hiebert-Murphy, D. (1992). Group treatment for child sexual abuse. *Canadian Psychology, 33,* 168–175.

Durrant, M. (1993). *Residential treatment: A cooperative, competency-based approach to therapy and program design.* New York: W.W. Norton & Co.

Frierich, W. N. (1991). *Casebook of sexual abuse treatment.* New York: W.W. Norton & Co.

Gil, E. (1991). *The healing power of play*. New York: The Guilford Press.

Hawkins, R. P., & Breiling, J. (1990). *Therapeutic foster care: Critical issues*. Washington, DC: Child Welfare League of America.

Hindman, J. (1989). *Just before dawn*. Ontario, OR: Alexandria Associates.

James, B. (1989). *Treating traumatized children: New insights and creative interventions*. Lexington, MA: Lexington Books.

Macaskill, C. (1991). *Adopting or fostering a sexually abused child*. London: B.T. Batsford Ltd.

Mather, C. L., & Debye, K. E. (1994). *How long does it hurt?* San Francisco: Jossey-Bass Publishers.

Meadowcroft, P., Tomlinson, B., & Chamberlain, P. (1994). Treatment foster care services: A research agenda for child welfare. *Child Welfare*, 73, 565–583

Meadowcroft, P., & Trout, B. A. (1990). *Troubled youth in treatment homes: A handbook of therapeutic foster care*. Washington, DC: Child Welfare League of America.

Monahan, C. (1993). *Children and trauma: A parent's guide for helping children heal*. Toronto, Ontario: Maxwell MacMillan Canada.

Montgomery, M. (1991). *Children's domestic abuse program*. Charlotte, NC: Kidsrights.

Pescosolido, F., & Petrella, D. (1986). The development, process, and evaluation of group psychotherapy with sexually abused preschool girls. *International Journal of Group Psychotherapy*, 36, 447–469.

Rutter, M. (1975). *Helping troubled children*. New York: Plenum Press.

Schafer, H. R. (1990). *Making decisions about children: Psychological questions and answers*. Oxford, UK: Blackwell.

Sgroi, S. (1982). *Handbook of clinical intervention in child sexual abuse*. Lexington, MA: Lexington Books.

Steinhauer, P. D. (1991). *The least detrimental alternative: A systematic guide to case planning and decision making for children in care*. Toronto, Ontario: University of Toronto Press.

Steinhauer, P. D. (1993). The contribution of child treatment professionals to children served by child protection agencies. *P.R.I.S.M.E.*, 3, 529–542.

Steward, M., Farqhuar, L., Dicharry, D., Glick, D., & Martin, P. (1986). Group therapy: A treatment of choice for young victims of child abuse. *International Journal of Group Psychotherapy, 36,* 261–277.

Sturkie, K. (1983). Structured group treatment for sexually abused children. *Health and Social Work, 8,* 299–308.

Trieschman, A., Whittaker, J.K., & Br endtro, L.K. (1969). *The other 23 hours: Child care work with emotionally disturbed children in a therapeutic milieu.* New York: Aldine de Gruyter.

Whittaker, J.K. (1979). *Caring for troubled children: Residential treatment in a community context.* San Francisco: Jossey-Bass Publishers.

5 Milieu-Based Treatment

Understanding Milieu-Based Treatment

In the previous chapters we examined the components of treatment for children who have been affected by sexual abuse. We explored the major therapeutic approaches, including individual psychotherapy and group work. Finally we reviewed the development and goals of a therapeutic milieu.

In this chapter we will trace the methods and techniques of milieu-based therapy. We will explore in more depth the stages an abused child moves through as she begins to recover inside the therapeutic milieu. We also provide charts (found in Appendix C) that highlight objectives in each stage, the tasks to be completed by the milieu-based therapist, and the skills required by the therapeutic caregiver to assist the sexually abused child within the milieu. By practicing these techniques and skills, a caregiver can turn a foster care environment into a therapeutic living space.

Also included in this chapter is the case example of "Allie and the Snake." This story illustrates what has been discussed in the first four chapters and demonstrates the sensitivity of the approach that the therapeutic caregiver uses and how that approach contributes to the child's ability to rethink and cope. The story also provides some sense of the child's perspective on behaviors that would seem puzzling and out of control to an adult who does not understand.

The Therapeutic Living Space

The treatment milieu offers the child an almost constant opportunity for learning, growth, and exploration. A highly skilled, milieu-based therapist looks after the child's basic care needs, and at the precise moment the child's need arises, the caregiver is able to turn basic care into a therapeutic moment. Thus, the events and discussions surrounding doing the dishes, playing a card game, arguing with a peer, having a bandage put on a cut, or having a feverish brow cooled by a wet cloth are all rich opportunities for considering the world (and the adults in it) in a new way.

For the child who has been sexually abused, the treatment milieu is a place where good things may happen. Individuals within the milieu relate to each other in ways she has never seen before. Adults have a way of understanding and talking to children that is frightening and intriguing at the same time—frightening because the adult is talking openly about things that were dark secrets at worst, and uncomfortable and embarrassing at best, intriguing because the adult seems to have an unusual depth of perception about what it is like to be and feel as this child does. These interactions invite the child to become a partner in solving problems.

Children's reactions to this place and these people are as varied as the children themselves. Sometimes children are resistant and hostile. They need to be supported to acknowledge the feelings they have resisted and channeled into acting out for so long. Others need patient understanding in order to express more directly the worries and discomforts they feel when they discuss difficult topics. Other children are stoic and silent; only the occasional nod signals that they are willing to have the adult continue to try to give a voice to the internal battle the child is waging. Other children seem to jump in with both feet, as if they have been waiting for a long time to get at these issues. Some will need to be slowed down and given some boundaries about the discussion, while others are truly ready to begin to explore and process.

The ways problems and issues are handled are at first hard to understand, but eventually children begin to view the adult as supportive and helpful. They begin to see themselves as surrounded by a kind of emotional sanctuary that, eventually, will allow them to do some important work.

This concept of "sanctuary" is all important. Sanctuary is a place where you feel safe and cherished. Each of us has our own special sanctuary. It might be in a church, sitting on the pew, looking at the windows or the cathedral roof, listening to the choir. It might be by a stream on a beautiful day, watching clouds scud overhead. It can be at a feast table, with candles lit and the faces of dear friends and family all around. Wherever it is, our sanctuary evokes feelings of safety, belonging, sharing, and laying down our burdens.

While we are always welcome and cherished in the sanctuary, it is not without its rules. We are not allowed to run up and down the aisles at religious services, for instance. That would spoil the sanctuary of others. The rules and demands of the sanctuary, however, are gently presented, taught with love and respect, forgiving of our human error, and patient in allowing us to learn at the pace we are able. True sanctuary never punishes, only encourages. It is a place of ultimate acceptance, understanding, forgiveness, and support. This is the state the child must feel within the milieu in order to take the first, hesitant step of sharing and working through the pain of the past.

Techniques in the Therapeutic Milieu

In the therapeutic milieu, the child's needs can be addressed at a number of different levels, in a number of different ways. In this section we will summarize some of the techniques most often used in the therapeutic milieu, and examine how they are helpful to children.

Structures, Rules and Anchor Points
Structure

A *therapeutic structure* is a carefully planned series of events, activities, and opportunities for choice making and relating that help guide a child through his or her day. The structure of the household in which the child lives is the basic, essential component needed to provide the child with the support she needs to begin to recover from the effects of abuse.

The structure provides predictability, comfort, and "ordinariness" to a child whose thoughts and feelings are often out of control. Without a clear structure the troubled child is prone to feeling anxious and out of control.

With a good structure in place, a sensitive caregiver can begin to anticipate those times in the day, or events in the week that will be stressful for the child. Instead of reacting to problems after the stress occurs, the caregiver can actually prevent problems by offering support and assistance to the child as the stressful period approaches.

Routines

A therapeutic structure is composed mainly of basic daily routines. Examples of routines are waking up, mealtimes, leaving for school, after school, the evening routine, and bedtime.

Children who have been traumatized are highly reactive to change and unpredictability, even in the daily routine. They do best when the basic daily schedule is stable and predictable; even the smallest changes can provoke reactions.

To be supportive, the daily routines must be developmentally appropriate, and highly consistent. The steps required to complete the routines should be done similarly each time. Change, when it is needed, must be anticipated, planned for, and often rehearsed in advance in order to avoid a behavioral crisis for the child.

Predictability in the caregiver's response within the structure is equally important. Traumatized children are extremely sensitive to adult moods and behavior, and highly likely to misinterpret adult intentions or meaning. Sudden changes in the way the adult seems to be handling things can lead to a feeling of being in danger, which results in behavioral escalations and blowups. In the most careful therapeutic environments, caregivers manage daily routines and solve problems in as predictable and unchanging a way as is realistically possible.

It is a challenge to offer this level of predictability within a family home. However, the better the caregivers are able to achieve predictability, the better the child will function. Anxiety levels will be reduced, the child's energy will not be as consumed by trying to anticipate and avoid danger, and the likelihood of being able to relax and become more trusting of an adult is increased.

Rules

Rules are the daily guidelines that help people in the therapeutic household feel safe and secure. Most households have rules. They serve the function of teaching norms and social behavior, and maintain harmony between family members.

In the therapeutic milieu, rules play an important role in establishing a setting where growth is possible. Rules act as a way to "contain" the child when she does not yet have internalized behavioral controls. They prevent violence and abusive contact and language, while promoting mutual respect and socially appropriate ways of having her needs met. They establish the environment as one in which important work is being done.

Rules become an important vehicle for assessing children's functioning and intervening in their emotional lives. When traumatized children break rules, this often presents an excellent opportunity for understanding the emotions underlying the behavior, looking at the consequences of the behavior, and learning to make better choices. In the therapeutic setting, consequences for breaking rules are not "punishment" as much as learning opportunities; consequences are therefore kept safe, respectful of the child, short lived, and educational.

Caregivers should develop a list of household rules about "being with one another." Rules might include guidelines on dress, touching, the kinds of issues that may be talked about and with whom, and who may be alone with whom. (See Appendix D, "House Rules About Being Safe.")

These rules are an important foundation for managing traumatized and abused children. Often children, who put a great deal of energy into sorting out the interactional signals that abuse might happen, are appreciative of a clear set of standards with which they can assess their own personal safety.

Rules for being with one another are usually developed in a family meeting. The caregiver brings up the importance of feeling safe and comfortable in this environment, and establishes the need for a set of "guidelines" for everyone to follow. Everyone contributes to developing a list of household rules that will contribute to a feeling of mutual well-being. Foster fathers find these discussions especially helpful in establishing safe limits in an open, straightforward way.

The resulting rules are clearly posted, regularly reviewed, and updated as each child arrives, or as events dictate.

Anchor Points

Anchor points is a term used to describe "touching base" opportunities built into the day. These times allow the adult to check on
how a child is functioning and to offer behavioral, emotional, or
problem-solving support and may include these occasions:
- A wake-up routine where the adult speaks quietly with the child
  for a few minutes before the day begins;
- An after-school routine, where the adult offers the child a snack
  and a chance to talk about the day's events;
- Just before supper time, when the adult can check on the child's
  emotional state after a period of interaction with peers; and
- The time after ending evening activities but before the bedtime routine.

These touch points are proactive and serve the function of allowing the adult to get a sense of the child's needs and offer support
long before a behavioral crisis occurs.

Behavioral Messages

Children often leave "behavioral messages" in structures, routines, and anchor points. If a child is upset and needs support, routines that are usually managed perfectly are suddenly missed, or
she refuses to participate in them. Obviously, the more predictable
the environment, the greater the chance that the caregiver will be
aware of a child's distress before an episode of escalating acting out
occurs.

Rather than becoming engaged in a power struggle over the routine, the milieu-based therapist understands that the child is signal-
ling that something is wrong and needs support. She is able to move
with a child and offer the intensive life space counseling that is
needed to help the child through a bad moment.

*Life Space Counseling**
Definition

Life space counseling is a term used to describe the concept of in-
terviewing children in a therapeutic milieu using a clinical ap-

---

* We have drawn heavily upon the work of Mary Wood and Nicholas
   Long for this section.

proach. Using many of the same ideas and methods as traditional psychotherapy, the concept of offering daily care in a therapeutic way has been in existence since the 1950s. The techniques of the life space interview have proved to be as useful in the treatment foster care environment as they have in traditional residential treatment settings.

The *life space* refers to the total environment surrounding the child in treatment—the physical, social, psychological, and cultural space in which the child lives. The focus of intervention takes place within this "space."

The "counseling" that goes on inside this life space surrounds the events, crisis, and problems that emerge within the milieu. The counseling adult learns to see a specific event through the eyes of the child. This event is then used as the beginning point for helping the child achieve new insights and learn important life lessons. These counseling sessions contribute to meeting the therapeutic goals for the child, and can happen several times a day.

Goals

The broad goals of life space counseling are as follows.

- Assist the child to understand life events:
    - Help her understand the part her personal behavior and feelings contribute to problems in daily living,
    - Help her learn to identify and appreciate the impact of her own actions on others,
    - Help her learn the consequences of her existing behavior on herself and others, and
    - Help her recognize alternatives that could have led to a more positive consequence.
- Improve the child's motivation to change:
    - Help her believe that change for the better is possible,
    - Help her build self-esteem so that she believes she deserves a better alternative, and
    - Help her build confidence to try something different.
- Offer the child a corrective relationship with adults:
    - Impress upon her that her perceptions and feelings are respected,

- Demonstrate that caring adults are able to recognize the individuality and qualities of children, and
- Provide experiences with adults who use power and control wisely and solve problems satisfactorily.

When children have the emotional support they need, including understanding and sensitivity to their feelings, they can be helped to give up problem behavior in favor of words. Then discussions with a supportive caregiver will help them learn to problem solve better, control impulses and feelings, make constructive decisions, deal with others in a positive way, and learn to live in a more socially "normal" way. The life space counseling technique uses events or "crisis" in the life space as the framework within which these skills and attitudes will be learned.

Technique

The life space counseling techniques are summarized in the following six "steps."

1. **Focus on the incident.** The caregiver focuses on a set of immediate events that led to the child's stress and helps the child to start to talk about the incident rather than be overwhelmed by feelings leading to behaviors.
2. **Clarifying and rationalizing.** The caregiver helps the child to tell her version of the incident in her own way, from her own point of view. As her emotional intensity decreases, the caregiver helps the child to find the words to express her feelings and ideas about the event. The child then works to understand her response, stress, and involvement.
3. **Finding the therapeutic opportunity.** The caregiver explores the child's associated feelings and anxieties until sufficient understanding has been reached to be able to concisely state the central issues. "You were angry at Francis because she was trying to control you. You hate to feel controlled, because it makes you feel powerless and weak. So you fought back. Have I got it just about right?"

    When the caregiver understands the issue to this degree, she can then decide what therapeutic opportunity exists in this event and what can be achieved in the course of this intervention. Following are some examples of therapeutic goals that might be selected:

- Assist the child to "see" reality in a more objective, less distorted way. ("I only saw or remembered part of the problem.")
- Make a dysfunctional or destructive behavior less comfortable for the child. By pointing out how the behavior functions and how the pleasure the behavior generates is "distorted," the process can increase the child's desire to change the behavior toward a more truly satisfying alternative. ("Maybe I've been tricking myself.")
- Assist the child to not feel burdened by a shame-filled, destructive self-image. Instead, support development of self-confidence, recognize positive qualities, and capitalize on strengths instead of succumbing to weakness. ("Even when my friends pressured me, I was able to make good choices and be kind to myself.")
- Teach the child more adaptive attitudes, values, and social skills. ("I have the right intentions. Please teach me how to talk to others better so I don't keep having the same problems.")

4. **Looking for alternatives.** The caregiver and child look together at the consequences of the child's behavioral choice and decide if the consequence was the "right" solution. Together they generate alternate ways of handling the problem. "Could you have told Francis you didn't appreciate how she was making you feel, and let her know that you felt controlled? Maybe you could have warned her that you would refuse to participate any longer if it kept up." In this step the caregiver and child are evaluating problem solving strategies and making prosocial decisions.

5. **Rehearsal.** The caregiver and child work together to rehearse the chosen solution, to get a "feel" of what it would be like. The caregiver can enter the "role play" to give practice opportunity. Together, they review whether this solution would have achieved better consequences.

6. **Getting back to normal.** The caregiver and child focus on shutting down this conversation and look at how the child can get back into the events of the day. Emotions are "closed down."

Any short-term consequences to the original behavior are dealt with at this time. Humor, congratulations, a quick plan for how to manage the next few minutes, are all possible ways of achieving this transition step.

Skills Required

Certain skills are essential for becoming a good life space counsellor.

- **The knack for "dispassionate compassion."** Successful counsellors learn how to keep their own emotional response under control, while at the same time demonstrating caring and empathy (but not pity) for the child.
- **Avoiding the temptation to give advice.** Expert life space counsellors do not offer endless advice on how to solve problems "better." Instead, they are able to draw from the child the thoughts and skills that she needs to become a better problem solver.
- **Holding basic beliefs about the worth of children**, their right to a protective and nurturing environment, and hope for a better future.
- **A motivation to guide and teach children** and the ability to make positive emotional connections with them.
- **The ability to help children discover** and successfully assume personal responsibility in a safe and guided way.

A course on counseling skills, high-caliber consultation/supervision, and a good book on the theory of life space intervention will be valuable tools. (See end notes for specific reading suggestions.)

Therapeutic Activities

The opportunity for enjoyable, fun time for fun's sake is an important component in the therapeutic milieu. Leisure time activities provide a release of energy and stress and an opportunity to refresh the spirit.

When recreation is approached in a planned, thoughtful way, it can also help a child work on a therapeutic goal. Because play is a child's natural mode of learning, it can be used to facilitate growth and address personal damage in a planned way. Areas of growth might include self-esteem, improved peer relationships and social skills, practice in making choices, learning positive use of leisure time as a life skill, stress reduction, development of fine and gross motor skills, and opportunities to experience competence.

As we have seen, traumatized children often have uneven developmental growth, and the ability to play is often underdeveloped. Caregivers will need to assess play skills and teach "how to play" as a part of the therapeutic recreation plan. Areas of investigation and planning will include the following:

- Child's developmental status;
- Child's interests, preferences, and experiences;
- Basic skills;
- Social development;
- Gross and fine motor, muscle, and physical development;
- Readiness for team or cooperative experiences;
- Ability to manage competitiveness; and
- Level of adult support needed to achieve success.

The selection of an appropriate recreation option to match the child's developmental status and needs is the first step in developing an appropriate therapeutic recreation plan.

There are several good therapeutic recreation books on the market which will be helpful in this area; samples are listed in the chapter end notes.

Therapeutic Stories

Children quite naturally use imaginative storytelling to work out problems or conflicts. Through "pretending," they are able to try out various solutions to problems; often they can develop useful metaphors (stories or parables) that allow them to work out complicated issues in a way that they can comfortably understand and manage.

Traumatized children often do not have this same ability. Their play might be restricted to reenacting traumatic events over and over. Often they do not seem to have developed the ability to use words (language) or ideas (symbols) that they need to think about old problems in new ways. For these children, listening to simple stories with powerful messages about the possibility of change, empowerment, and healing can introduce a whole new way of thinking about problems. "Therapeutic stories" are designed for use by therapists to introduce positive ideas about problem solving.

These stories are like "fables," where characters are confronted with difficult situations. By finding courage, or achieving new insights, or standing up for themselves in some new way, the characters learn about their own strengths and their own ability to survive difficult situations. These stories can be used successfully in the therapeutic milieu. They can be particularly effective when used in a special one-to-one time between a younger child and a caregiver.

In one application, the caregiver reads aloud the story and then offers the child an art medium (clay, drawing, colors) with which to illustrate the story. They can draw or make any part of the story they would like, or anything that seems right to make. The adult and the child can then talk about the characters in the story, exploring how the characters might have felt, or why they made certain choices. Together they will review the child's artwork and talk about the use of color. This technique can be particularly useful when there is access to art therapy consultation.

Later, the caregiver can use the metaphor of the story as a suggestion for solutions to problems that occur in daily living. ("Remember what the bunny did?") Stories about themes of empowerment can be particularly useful in helping a child begin to establish her right not to be victimized.

The Power of Family Living

Productive and satisfying relationships are effectively modelled in foster and residential care on a daily basis. The chance to experience these kinds of relationships through observation is a safe, non- threatening way of learning. The child can see firsthand appropriate communication, effective coping with stress, assertiveness, and functional gender relationships. The child can also gain further therapeutic benefit by participating in conversations about her observations about how others' relationships are unfolding.

It is particularly important for abused children to participate in relationships in a nonabusive family setting. In these settings, relationships are not based on secrets, coercion, abuse of role or authority, or power based on the commodity of sexuality. Instead the relationships are based on mutual respect and true affection. This provides the child with new ways of thinking about family relationships, parenting, and mutuality in relationships that may have an impact on her future choices as partner, parent, and family member.

Stages of Healing in the Milieu

As we have seen, treatment of the aftermath of sexual abuse requires a broad-based approach. The quality and richness of interrelationships, the absence of harm, and exposure to remedial day-to-day experiences are essential to the healing process.

Another part of the healing process is the telling of the child's personal "story." The story is not just about the abuse, but about her life, her memories, her trauma, and her triumphs. Her story is what has happened to her and who she is because of it. There is not one single story, but a variety of stories and incidents that emerges in bits and pieces as she tests the safety of the environment and the reliability of relationships.

The telling of the "story" should not be the focus of work until the caregiver feels that the whole child has been acknowledged and accepted. If the child never chooses to tell her story, it should not be seen as a failure on the caregiver's part. The child will deal with her story when she is ready, not on a schedule (perhaps not until well into adulthood). Nor is the telling of the story a magical cure. Instead it is one tool in a thoughtful, helping strategy.

The child's work on her story can be roughly viewed as occurring in three stages: the period before the child has told her full story, the period during which she is struggling with the telling of her story and all of the terror and pain that comes with it, and the period after disclosure, when the child is attempting to "get on with living" as a less affected person. These stages do not have simple, clear divisions with progressive movement from one to another. There is frequent regression and moving forward in an uneven way. The framework does, however, give caregivers a starting point and a way of organizing what is happening in the child's inner world. The stages are described in more detail in the following sections.

The Prestory Phase

In this stage, the child has not yet fully disclosed and has not begun to deal with the impact of abuse. For example, she may just have experienced the crisis of her original disclosure and seen the devastating effect of the breakup of her family and her own admission into a therapeutic setting. At this point, the child is introduced to the therapeutic milieu, works on settling in, and begins the long process of developing enough trust to go further in her personal healing.

In the meantime, the story of the abuse is "told" over and over again, lived out in the pain, behavior, worries, and ideas the child carries about with her. The sometimes-puzzled milieu-based therapist has the task of responding appropriately to these hard-to-read behavioral messages at the same time as bringing the child's most self-destructive and problematic behaviors under control.

The Story Phase

In this phase the child has come to believe that she is safe enough from harm that she can risk telling her story. In a slow, painful manner, filled with testing behaviors, riddled with apparent breakthroughs only to be followed by regressions, the child struggles to remember and communicate what has happened to her. Following each communication she struggles with the fear that her caregiver may need to reject her; she finds ways of asking the question, "How do you see me now?"

This child is extremely vulnerable, easily overwhelmed by memories or fears, and she easily shuts down. She is struggling to cope with an enormous amount of stress, having available only those fragile coping mechanisms she was able to develop in the abusive environment.

The child may feel angry with the caregiver for "making" her tell. The testing behaviors that follow and continue to follow with every new piece of the story can feel frustrating to the caregiver. ("Doesn't she know by now that I can be trusted?") As each part of the story emerges, the caregiver may struggle to see that anything new is being said, while it is obvious from the child's reaction that this seemingly similar story has a different and important meaning for the child. It is hard not to view all of this reaction as a personal betrayal. The caregiver will need to struggle not to communicate frustration to the child and to find personal relief in her own support system.

Since a great deal of work and effort goes into getting to and through the story phase, the emergence of the child's ability to tell her story may feel like a victory for the therapist. If it does not happen, she may mistakenly feel like a failure. The danger for the caregiver is to become overinvested in the story and not attend to the whole child with the understanding that there are many aspects of the milieu-based relationship that are just as important to healing.

The Poststory Phase

Once the story has been told, the child and caregiver need to determine "where to go from here." The child may have come to believe there was magic in the telling, and when nothing happens, relationships are the same, or personal relief is not forthcoming, disappointment follows. She will need to work through these feelings.

Moving on requires that child and caregiver struggle together toward healing. Understanding the personal impact of the abuse and the connections between the abuse and her present decisions, exploring the steps toward personal empowerment, and decision making are part of this phase. The child begins to understand that the behaviors she has relied on to keep her safe are no longer functional. She begins to understand that her former "self" is changing. She may need to work through some resentment about this before she is open to the opportunity to develop new relationships.

In this stage the child, who presented for so long as suffering from poor self-esteem and lack of empowerment, begins to emerge as a competent individual who is able to make conscious choices. Even when those choices are not good ones, they are hers, and she is able to own them. The caregiver/therapist at this stage is a helpmate, teacher, and guide. Each day's events offer rich opportunities for exploration, problem solving, learning, and self-correction. The milieu-based therapist offers both role modeling and a testing ground for a newly found and maturing self. Often children are not ready to make use of the trauma assessment tool until they have entered this stage (see page 30).

Milieu-Based Therapeutic Tasks

Stage of Growth

The tables in Appendix C are designed to allow the milieu-based therapist to pinpoint the stage of healing the child is in. Of course children do not travel "neatly" from one phase of progress to another. Growth can be very uneven, and caregivers should expect setbacks. However, by looking at the "phases" as broad sequences, we can understand what kind of work might be going on for the child at any given point in time.

Therapeutic Objectives

Once we have more or less accurately located the stage, we can look at the objectives that guide our work in each of the stages. These objectives act as therapeutic "agendas," or a list of what needs to be done to support the child during the stages of development.

Tasks of the Therapeutic Caregiver

The therapist then breaks the therapeutic objectives down into the broad tasks for the caregiver to work toward during each phase. The tasks help to focus the milieu-based therapist's efforts and act as a checkpoint to return to when the work seems to lose focus, change directions, or appears overly complicated.

The tasks may be few in number and remarkably simple, considering the complexity of the problems to be addressed. The caregiver should always keep in mind that the therapeutic milieu is the key component that allows this model to work. In a well-planned, highly supportive milieu, most ordinary life events have already been maximized for learning opportunities. Optimally, little occurs accidentally and therapeutic, or teaching moments, occur frequently throughout the day.

The skilled milieu-based therapist can maximize the opportunities for careful observation and sensitive responses within the 24-hour milieu, so that the child is surrounded by a continuous source of supportive feedback. The trick is in pacing, allowing the child to take the lead on the topic of abuse, while the caregiver takes the lead on the issues of daily living.

Skills Required

The skills that are required to successfully support a child through the healing process are different at each stage of the child's development. They become progressively more complex, ranging from tolerance and behavior management skills at the beginning, through counseling skills, and finally into launching and termination skills. The caregiver will need these skills over a period of years, not weeks and months.

For the milieu-based therapist to be truly effective, she will need to accurately appraise what her current skill level is, sort out where the stumbling blocks are likely to be, and make an active plan for skill building. The caregiver will need help from the supporting agency and clinical team in order to have access to the training and supervision required to build and practice new skills. Finally, a strong plan for supervising implementation, which allows for ongoing refinements and corrections to occur, is essential.

"Training" in this form of work is anything but a "one-shot" enterprise. It is a serious investment in skill development, the rewards of which will be a caregiver who is a skilled guide in a healing process for very damaged children. At the end of this chapter is a case example that illustrates various points from Chapters 1 through 4. It also shows how the caregiver can sensitively respond to the child using information in this chapter.

A Final Thought

Living with and treating a traumatized child is a great challenge. It can be disheartening, exhausting, and overwhelming. When the child reaches breakthroughs in understanding, however, all the hard times are quickly forgotten. There are few jobs we can put ourselves to that offer the same kind of deep satisfaction as milieu-based treatment.

Case Example

Allie and the Snake: A Story

Allie put her bag down on the bed. She leaned over and pushed on it a couple of times, feeling its spring. A new bed. A new place, new people, new rules, new things to be afraid of. Allie felt tears coming to her eyes, but forced them back. "I won't cry. Nothing can make me feel." She pulled her mouth into a practiced smile, one that she did not mean, and headed down the stairs to join her new (and improved?) foster mother.

Until a few hours ago Allie was the foster child of Mabel and Tom Smith. Allie thought that Mabel would always be there for her. She was wrong. She made a choice to trust someone and show her just a little bit of the pain inside, and look what happened. Mabel threw her out. Allie had heard Mabel talk to the worker about her.

"She goes into huge screaming fits. She tears the house apart. Last night she tore apart her bed and threw it down the stairs. I have to hold her and rock her while she cries and screams, hour after hour. She has gouged me with her nails, blackened my eyes, bumped my nose with her head. I can't take it anymore. I'm a mess, she's a mess."

And so Allie packed her things and moved on.

She didn't have the words to explain what happened. Her new therapist, Dr. Will, was asking her to play with the toys in his room. She knew what he was after. He wanted her to talk. "Oh, God, I can't talk. But playing isn't the same as talking. I wasn't told I couldn't. So I will play it out a little."

But then she had to go home with all of the smells in her nose, the touch of his hands, the feel of his saliva on her lips. And the bed. He was there on the bed. It needed to go down the stairs.

"Please, take it away, I can't see this. I can't talk. I'll die if I talk."

But all that would come out were screams. And so Allie packed her things. And moved on. "I'm sorry, Mabel. I couldn't talk. I wasn't allowed to talk."

Allie walked into the kitchen. Mrs. Ernest was there.

"Hello, Allie. Did you have a chance to see your room?"

"Yes," said Allie.

"I wonder what it must be like for a young kid like you to come to a strange house. To see a strange room. To touch a strange bed. I wonder if it wouldn't be kind of scary."

Allie looked at her strangely. What was she saying? Of course she was scared. You didn't need to be a genius to figure that out.

"Uh huh," said Allie.

"It's hard to talk when you don't know what to say. It's hard to feel like it's OK to talk. I wonder what it's like for you, to feel that things are so hard?"

Confused now, Allie wondered for a minute if Mrs. Ernest really knew. No, she couldn't. But this grown-up sure had a weird way of talking.

Mrs. Ernest went on to explain the house rules. You aren't allowed to walk around in pajamas without a house coat on. That was because they wanted people to feel safe. Some of the children in the house didn't like to be touched. Mr. Ernest worried about touch, too, she said, because he wondered sometimes if touch was confusing for the girls. Mr. Ernest had a rule that touching was OK as long as they talked about touch first, and figured out what was going to be a good touch, and what was going to feel like a bad touch.

"It's very important to feel safe here, Allie. You'll find we talk a lot about how to stay safe, how to feel like we have control over what happens to us. I wonder what that will be like for you, to talk so much about being safe. Will it feel very different to you?"

What's safe? thought Allie. What are you talking about? She shrugged her shoulders.

"Uh huh," said Allie.

That night Allie lay in her new bed. She lay stiff as a board and tried to take up as little space on the bed as possible. Just enough not to fall off. Maybe falling off would bring an adult in. A scary adult. An adult that touched children in pajamas. Finally she fell asleep.

Mrs. Ernest went downstairs and spoke to Mr. Ernest. "Howard," she said, "She sleeps like a board. She's lying right on the edge of the bed. I wonder how on earth she managed to fall asleep at all. We'll have to work on how to make her feel safer at bedtime. There must be something that she can tell me about bedrooms that can help us make it feel like a less traumatic place to go."

Over the next several months, Allie must have heard the word "safe" a million times. She was even starting to use it herself. She spent so much time thinking about how to be safe, what would make her feel safe, that she was almost beginning to believe that she was safe. She remembered her first week, how Mrs. Ernest, Sue, talked about making the bedroom her own, special safe place where it would feel good to go. She turned her bed into a couch, with Sue making matching pillows and something she called "bolsters." They made curtains, too. Soft, fluffy curtains that looked like they were for a girl. Allie wondered how Sue was so smart. She still didn't like going to sleep, but at least it wasn't a bed.

The first time that Allie had one of her remembering times, she was scared to death. She tried not to scream, honestly she did. She breathed and breathed. She tried closing her eyes, but the pictures came too fast, and she started to feel sick. She opened her mouth and the screaming started. The other kids in the house all ran off. Allie started to hit and punch and kick. Then she heard a voice.

"Allie, it's Sue. You are right here, safe with me. Good girl, Allie, you're here with me now. No one can touch you, and no one can hurt you. You are safe. And you are right here with me."

Allie stopped screaming and kicking. She looked around. The pictures were gone. All she could hear was Sue's voice, Sue's amazing voice.

"Boy, you were really working hard there, Allie. You were breathing so hard. I wonder what was happening that made it important for you to work so hard. And scream so hard. You have a good set of lungs, girl!"

They laughed together. Allie tried to answer Sue's question. It was awful. It was overwhelming. It was terrifying. It was here. It was now.

"Sick," said Allie.

"Yes, it looked as if it might be a sick thing. You were a brave girl, Allie. You fought and fought the sick, and now you're here safe with me. Good for you, honey. You had a bad time, but you came through it."

"I did, didn't I?" thought Allie. "I didn't lose me. I pulled back." And she smiled, a real smile, for the first time in a very long time. "But be careful," she told herself. "This one might be the smartest one of all. You can't afford to trust."

By Christmas, Allie's play at Dr. Will's place was getting boring. She knew she had told her story over and over, and she knew nothing bad was going to happen if you played out your story. She knew she was safe. Until you start to talk you are safe. But when you talk the bad things happen. Except that now Allie wasn't so sure. "Sue says I talk with my actions," she thought. "Sometimes Sue wonders what my actions mean. She guesses sometimes, and sometimes she's so close it must be almost like talking. And I'm still safe."

One day Allie decided to test it.

"Sue, what happens if a little girl is not safe, and she tells about it? What if the unsafe thing can come and hurt the little girl?"

"It's important to you that I understand that telling about scary things might hurt the little girl. I wonder what it is that the little girl thinks might happen?"

"The snake will eat her."

"Hmmm, the snake will eat her. That is an important thing. It must be hard to think about telling if the little girl believes a snake will hurt her. But how does she know about the snake?"

"Her daddy told her."

"Oh, her daddy told her. Her daddy told her that if she talked about the not-safe thing a snake would eat her. Did the little girl believe her daddy?"

Allie stopped, stunned. Of course she believed her daddy. "Of course I believed my daddy. Believe. Why did I believe him? Is it true? Is there a snake?"

"I wonder what you're thinking about now, Allie. Could it be that a grown-up person would tell a little girl a scary story like the snake story just to keep her from talking? What would it mean if there was no snake?"

It would mean I could talk, thought Allie. It would mean I could tell Sue about it.

Allie struggled for a long time with the idea of the snake. She was remembering and remembering. Sometimes she yelled and fought and screamed so hard that she was afraid Sue would tell her to go. But Sue was always calm. She was always wondering. Allie began to believe that Sue already knew and was just waiting. And so she told. And the snake did not eat her.

It was hard for Allie to remember that young child. She had come so far. How stupid to believe there was a snake inside her that would eat her. What a jerk he was to tell her that. What a lousy way to keep a little kid shut up. But sometimes, in the wee small hours, she could still remember what it felt like to touch herself, feeling for the snake, hoping it would not hurt her.

So many parts of her had been touched by the lies. It was hard to know when she was making good decisions and when she was making decisions like a little girl who was hurt. One day she had gotten really mad at Sue for calling her a hurt little girl.

"Allie, why is it you decided not to go into the piano competition? You really love to play, and you've really worked hard. Your teacher thought you were ready!"

"I would never be able to win. It's useless. And I don't want all of those people looking at me."

"Whose decision was that, Allie? Was it the young woman who is competent and alive, or was it the little girl inside who was hurt and who can't let herself feel good about herself?"

"Drop dead, Sue!" Allie had screamed.

But Sue had been right. It was her little girl who didn't want to. Who was afraid she was not good enough and was sure that others could see her pain. And of course, she knew that was not possible. Later she apologized to Sue.

"You were right, it was the little girl inside who had made the decision, Sue. She was afraid and unsure, and for a minute she was sure everyone would be able to see the damage."

Allie decided not to go into the piano competition, but because she was not yet ready to face that kind of pressure without being too hard on herself. She had soothed the little girl inside one more time, and simultaneously made a good decision for the young adult she was becoming.

Recommended Readings

Beeler, N. G., Rycus, J. S., & Hughes, R. C. (1990). *The effects of abuse and neglect on child development: A training curriculum.* Washington, DC: Child Welfare League of America.

Briere, J. N. (1992). *Child abuse trauma: Theory and treatment of the lasting effects.* Newbury Park, CA: Sage Publications.

Brohl, K. (1996). *Working with traumatized children: A handbook for healing.* Washington, DC: CWLA Press.

Burns, M. (1993). *Time in: A handbook for child and youth care professionals.* Toronto, Ontario: Burns-Johnston Publishing.

Crisci, G., Lay, M., & Lowenstein, L. (1997). *Paper dolls and paper airplanes: Therapeutic exercises for sexually traumatized children.* Charlotte, NC: Kidsrights.

Davis, N. (1990). *Once upon a time: Therapeutic stories to heal abused children.* Oxon Hill, MD: Psychological Associates of Oxon Hill.

Durrant, M. (1993). *Residential treatment: A cooperative, competency-based approach to therapy and program design.* New York: W.W. Norton & Co.

Frierich, W. N. (1991). *Casebook of sexual abuse treatment.* New York: W.W. Norton & Co..

Gil, E. (1991). *The healing power of play.* New York: The Guilford Press.

Hindman, J. (1989). *Just before dawn.* Ontario, OR: Alexandria Associates.

James, B. (1989). *Treating traumatized children: New insights and creative interventions.* Lexington, MA: Lexington Books.

Macaskill, C. (1991). *Adopting or fostering a sexually abused child*. London: B.T. Batsford Ltd.

Mather, C. L., & Debye, K. E. (1994). *How long does it hurt?* San Francisco: Jossey-Bass Publishers.

Monahan, C. (1993). *Children and trauma: A parent's guide for helping children heal*. Toronto, Ontario: Maxwell MacMillan Canada.

Parry, A., & Doan, R. E. (1994). *Story re-visions: Narrative therapy in the post modern world*. New York: Guilford Press.

Redl, F. (1972). The concept of a therapeutic milieu. In G.H Weber and B.J. Haberleinn (Eds.), *Residential treatment of emotionally disturbed children*. New York: Behavioral Publications.

Rutter, M. (1975). *Helping troubled children*. New York: Plenum Press.

Sgroi, S. (1982). *Handbook of clinical intervention in child sexual abuse*. Lexington, MA: Lexington Books.

Trieschman, A., Whittaker, J. K., & Brendtro, L. K.. (1969). *The other 23 hours: Child care work with emotionally disturbed children in a therapeutic milieu*. New York: Aldine de Gruyter.

van der Kolk, B. (1995). *Counting the cost*. Video. Nevada City, CA: Cavalcade Productions, Inc.

Whittaker, J. K. (1979). *Caring for troubled children: Residential treatment in a community context*. San Francisco: Jossey-Bass Publishers.

Wood, M. M., & Long, N. J. (1991). *Life space intervention: Talking with children and youth in crisis*. Austin, TX: PRO-ED Inc.

6 Challenges in the Therapeutic Milieu

This chapter presents some of major themes and relationship or behavioral challenges that play a role in the milieu-based approach.

The Effects of Working Through Abuse on the Caregiver

The milieu is based on healing relationships—one of the greatest resources a milieu has to offer a child. In its strength, however, lies its weakness. In the effort to help the child through the difficult period of healing, the therapeutic caregiver may sometimes disregard her own reactions to the child's trauma. While mobilizing all her resources to focus on the child, her own strong feelings and reactions can gradually build up. These feelings need to be acknowledged and attended to. Otherwise, the accumulation of guilt, impatience, sadness, rage, disgust, and anxiety can create havoc in the caregiver's own life, as well as contaminating her relationship with the child. This focus on keeping yourself healthy and whole in the face of outstandingly challenging work is equally important for all therapists working in this area of specialty.

Developmentally Appropriate Responses

The power of revisiting and dealing with a trauma can disrupt the child's psychological balance. It is normal for a traumatized child to look and act like a younger child for a period of time. Such regression may be necessary in the moment and is not something the child should be "talked out of" or discouraged from doing. "Babyish" behavior should therefore not lead to consequences, with the exception of those behaviors that are having a negative impact on placement viability. We cannot emphasize enough the importance of "listening" to the child's needs rather than the caregiver's own expectations. When the caregiver anticipates behavioral and emotional regression, she can match her responses to the child who is acting as if she were younger for a time. The result will be a greater sense of security on the part of the child, and a deepening of the child's ability to trust this adult who seems so responsive to her hidden, inner self. In this case the behavior may be given up when it is no longer needed.

Repetitious Retelling of Traumatic Events

It is not the norm for children to retell their stories over and over again in the daily living environment. Indeed, a repetitive telling of the circumstances of the abuse can actually be further traumatizing to the child. When a child seems "stuck" in telling her story and seems to be achieving no relief in the retelling, this is usually a sign that something is not happening to make the retelling a healing experience. Such retelling can fuel unproductive anger, revenge fantasies, or even the beginnings of the thought that the child's own behaviors are never wrong. Thinking becomes stuck at the point of looking at blame and never moves to resolution. The whole basis for the child's creation of a new reality for herself gets missed.

Often, when such a state occurs, it is because the child has not yet attended to some fundamental piece of work. The caregiver can help the child by helping her identify which aspects of the work remain unattended. Some areas for examination are listed below:

• Giving up her idea of fantasy relationships inside a fantasy family,
• Giving up her wish to be a part of the abusive family,
• Giving up her investment in sanitizing (reducing the horror of the facts) in order to protect other family members, and
• Beginning to deal with the grief and pain of the separation and loss of the family.

Sometimes retelling of the abuse is prompted by some life event or developmental stage that makes the events of the past take on new meaning. Such retelling makes the story of the child's abuse relevant in the here and now. For instance, she may be reacting to a new developmental challenge (e.g., has a boyfriend for the first time) or a significant event in her life (e.g., a parent dies, the perpetrator is released from jail, or another child is born to the family). In these instances retelling is not a reenactment, but a reprocessing and coming to terms in a new way. Through this kind of retelling, the child may experience a progressive relief.

In the therapeutic milieu, the child can participate in an accepting emotional sanctuary where the retelling of the story is understood as a part of the healing process. The caregiver's role as another therapist on the child's treatment team helps her to be able to offer the child the accepting listening ear she needs.

Hearing the story of the abuse over and over is often difficult to tolerate for the caregiver, who has begun to feel protective toward and emotionally invested in the child. Stories of sexual abuse can be devastating. If the verbal or nonverbal message given to the child is that the story is too overwhelming or too scary for the caregiver to handle, the child will likely retreat and miss out on the chance to heal by finally getting all of the pain converted to words. Good supports will need to be available to the adult caregivers in order to work through the personal impact, so that the appropriate therapeutic stance can be maintained.

Behavioral Responses

Behaviors may escalate as the child begins to relive and struggle to work out the past trauma. The essence of trauma, from the child's perspective, is a loss of control. The child feels powerless, unable to protect herself from unwanted intrusion and is not convinced that abuse will not happen again, even in this supposedly "safe" environment. As a way of regaining at least a small level of control over her own existence, the child is compelled to test out the motivation, intent, behaviors, and reliability of caring adults over and over again. Behaviors that come with the struggle to regain control might include testing behaviors, noncompliance, aggression, tantrums, manipulation, etc.

The caregiver in the therapeutic milieu expects and processes testing behaviors as a part of helping the child work toward becoming a survivor. The caregiver will need to respond with caring and

"Jen has been misbehaving so much lately. I have to tell you, I'm getting discouraged."

"Tell me, what has she been doing."

"The thing that is worrying me most right now is that she repeatedly stays out overnight. I'll get a phone call in the morning, sometimes even the night before, but she knows I hate it."

"Do you have any sense of why she is doing it?"

"Yeah, I think it's about control. I have control over so many parts of her life, this is one way to get it back."

"And yet she calls you to let you know she's safe."

"Yeah, a polite control freak."

"What do you think she might be asking you with her behavior?"

"Oh, I don't know. Will you let me go? Will you reject me if I do this thing you hate? Will you try to bring me back? Can I trust you to do the right thing? Can I have control over me? Maybe all of them."

"Same old theme, huh? Testing, one, two, three. Can I trust you with important things about me?"

"Oh, geez, another test to see if she can share some part of her story. She has been testing me so long. Hasn't it been enough yet? Doesn't she know she can trust me yet?"

"Apparently not. Let's have a look at what the tests have been lately, and see if we can find any pattern here. Maybe she's telling us something and we just haven't gotten the message yet..."

This conversation between treatment foster parent Mrs. Bell and her supervising social worker, John, is typical of the support worker/foster parent team relationship.

---

supportive messages while still maintaining the limits and rules of the house.

A human response to living with the sexually abused child is frustration that, after repetitive, thorough, and extensive testing, the child is still not assured that the caregiver is safe and trustworthy. Since such tests are important to establishing a true trust relationship, and because the child has such difficulty with trust in any form, the tests are likely to go on for some time, and even need to be repeated as new stages of treatment are reached. The caregiver will need support to cope with her own personal frustration with testing that seems never ending and the child's slowness in responding to good intervention.

Rules and limits are comforting for children, in that they create some predictability in an out-of-control world. Rules need to be firm but fair (indeed, fairness is an extremely important theme). While predictability in the rules is very important, as the child grows she also needs to learn to speak up on her own behalf. Therefore caregivers always need to be open to emotionally appropriate "negotiation" as part of establishing the supportive environment.

A behavior modification approach with this population may actually be counterproductive. As a general rule, the effective milieu-based therapeutic response understands that the child's behavior has a meaning. Once it is understood why the behavior exists, the child can be supported to give it up in exchange for a more productive response. There are, of course, exceptions. When children are in crisis a strong behavioral approach, such as a token economy, is often quite helpful, and the earliest days of any new placement are often eased with a clear behavior program. In the long run, however, it is far more effective to utilize some of the other therapeutic responses discussed in this book.

The Importance of Predictability

A predictable environment takes on new importance for the sexually abused child undergoing intensive therapy. This is not the time to be introducing the child to something new and different. Dealing with a trauma, which is by definition unusual, may make the "usual and ordinary" particularly comforting.

Caregivers can sometimes be tempted to create special events or "surprises" that are meant to please and distract the child who is working so hard to process her trauma. When these backfire because the child is unable to tolerate the stress of the change, disappointments and misinterpretations can occur. "Treats" for being compliant were likely a part of the abuse. While this time the intentions are good, the child may not be in a position to tell the difference, and her sense of safety may be affected.

Therefore, when the milieu-based therapist feels she would like to offer the child a healthy, stimulating recreational experience (and

At 6 years of age, Janet had a question she could not answer. "Why did my mommy marry Ivan when she knew Ivan was hurting me? Why did she pick him instead of me?" This question occurred every time there was a phone call, every time there was a supervised visit with mom. Joan, her treatment foster mother, waited for the right moment:

"Boy, Janet, you just think and think about that question. It is very important for you to have the answer."

"I want to know. Why did my mommy do that?"

"Yes, you want to know. Have you thought of any answers?"

"Me?

"Yes. Why do you think mommy did that."

"Maybe she didn't know Ivan was hurting me."

"Oh, I'm confused, I thought she did know."

"Yeah. I told her."

"That must be very very hard. You told her, but she married Ivan anyway."

"She should know better. I hate her. I hate her, hate her. "

"Mum should have known better. You told her, and she should have picked you, but she didn't, and that makes you mad. Can you think of any reason why she would do that, Janet?"

"She doesn't like me."

---

such experiences need to be offered frequently), then the experience must not be contingent on how well she is working on her issues. For the severely abused child, good behavior should not be required in order to enjoy a good experience. The good experiences are healing in and of themselves, and they need to form a good portion of the treatment approach. A child's behaviors, however, should inform the *kinds* of events that are chosen.

The caregiver does need to provide for healthy physical outlets and carefully choose activities that are fun and encourage positive interaction and the development of good social skills. These "therapeutic activities" do not need to be specially designed or selected. Any of the activities children enjoy in family settings can be therapeutic. The key is in selecting activities at which the child is likely to succeed.

"Oh, one reason might be because of how she felt about you. Maybe. Could there be another reason that has nothing to do with you?"

"I think she was very lonely. I think she wanted Ivan to be her friend first."

"Mum was lonely and needed Ivan to be her friend. So she married him. What is it like for you that mum married Ivan and you are in care?"

"I'm mad, mad, mad! Mum should have picked me. So there!"

"You are sure mad. If I were a little girl in care whose Mum married the man who hurt me, I think I would feel mad, too. And scared about what will happen to me. And sad. Very, very sad. It's hard to think that Mum did not pick you. You are a very wonderful girl. It would be easy to pick you. Mum must have been very, very lonely."

"Yes. She cried, you know."

"She cried?"

"When I told her. She called the Children's Aid, and then she cried."

"Why was she crying, do you think?"

"I don't know. I can't get inside my mother's head! Can I go now?" Joan let her go. For today, Janet had taken a big step. There were many steps to go, but the first one had been taken.

Considerations should include skill level (physical and social); ability to interact with others (short periods or long, closely supervised by adults or unsupervised); ability to tolerate rules and structures (complicated interactive games versus running along a beach, hiking in the woods); and developmental level (emotional, social, as well as age). A good book on therapeutic play, or a therapeutic recreation specialist, may be helpful in planning activities for these children.

Opportunities to Talk About Feelings

Talking about feelings can be difficult for any child, but is especially so for those who have been victimized by sexual abuse. The child will likely have been told by the abuser that talking about what has happened will have dire consequences, either for the child or someone she cares about. Also, many of her efforts to talk about her feelings in the past may have been ignored, disbelieved, or explained away as fantasy or dreams. "Talking" is therefore a dangerous activity. If the child's fledgling attempts to verbalize are hampered in any way by the caregiver, the child will quickly abandon verbalization and employ another coping strategy, such as acting out behaviorally.

The caregiver in the therapeutic milieu can offer a highly beneficial support by simply acknowledging the child's feelings. The feelings the child expresses are indeed terrible. The wise milieu therapist, however, does not try to "clean up" or sanitize the child's feelings. Instead she gives strong messages that all of the child's feelings, thoughts, and ideas are acceptable in the therapeutic milieu, and provides supportive responses that are suitable to the child's developmental level and in the child's language. She assures the child that her strong emotions will not destroy either the child or the milieu-based caregiver.

Children who have been traumatized often are not in touch with their own emotions. Feelings have been compressed, so that all strong negative emotion comes out, for instance, as anger. A helpful aspect of the therapeutic milieu is that, through discussion, modeling, or even more concrete interventions such as creation of a Feelings Scrapbook, caregivers can offer children highly supportive opportunities for sorting out and labeling feelings. The focus is on helping children to discover that their feelings are normal and to be able to access the full range of their emotions.

Fear is one of the most common feelings following an abusive experience. The traumatized child in the therapeutic milieu often presents as highly anxious, reactive, and easily frightened. Irrational connections or cause-effect relationships can be seen at play in day-to-day behavior, interfering with normal functioning. Examples can include such ordinary things as being afraid to close the bathroom door or sleep without a light on, or the unusual, such as refusing to drink milk or eat certain foods or refusing to walk into rooms of a certain color because of what the child is reminded of.

It is difficult for caregivers to see children experience this level of crippling fear. The temptation is to try to take the child's fear away. Ignoring the fears, or talking them away, arguing that there is nothing to be afraid of, or appealing to the child to be brave in the face of the fear, thereby conquering it, are all understandable responses. They are, however, not helpful.

A much more useful approach begins with an adult who can accept and respect a child's fears as reasonable in light of the child's experiences. Simply acknowledging that the child might be feeling a little (or a lot) afraid, and suggesting that the child need not face the fear alone is an important first step.

If the caregiver can communicate respect for the child's fear and willingness to act as an ally, then the child will be in a better position to accept adult support in processing the fear. Together, adult and child can review the issues that underlie the fear and sort through what kinds of supports or changes might be helpful in dealing with it. The child will need gentle suggestions of practical ways to deal with the fears without suggesting that the fear is unwarranted. Children supported in this manner are more likely to become truly "courageous" than those who are not given permission to deal with their fear appropriately.

Distortions and Misunderstandings

In order to establish meaning in her world, the child may have created a way of understanding relationships and events based on misunderstanding, misinterpretation, or distorted logic. To the outside observer, such distortions seem nonsensical. But in the child's inner world, the distortion has logic and helps her make the world more predictable.

For instance, the child may attempt to find the cause of the abuse in her own misdeeds. She may have concocted curious and improbable ways of keeping herself safe following the abuse. She may need to believe that her own magical thinking serves to protect her. A child might think that if she behaves "just right" and according to the rules of conduct the abuser has given her, she may be able to prevent the abuse.

The therapeutic caregiver will seek to understand the distortions the child has developed. She will not attempt to change the child's ideas through imposing her own views of reality, but will help the child explore her views. The milieu-based therapist understands that the child's distortions will eventually be corrected in one of two ways: either the child will experience things in a new way (i.e., I can feel close to someone without it becoming sexualized) that will affect her on an emotional level, or she will begin to think about things in a new way (wearing pink clothes does not mean I will be abused). Both kinds of changes are useful, and both may be offered within the therapeutic milieu.

Triggers and Anniversary Reactions

Calendar-related events, such as holidays, birthdays, or family gatherings, are normally happy events that we look forward to. Unfortunately, these events can trigger strong memories of abuse in a child. Events that seem innocent to the caregiver may trigger intrusive and painful memories for the child. For example, the sight of a Santa Claus suit may trigger flashbacks of being abused by a drunken relative similarly attired one Christmas.

The therapeutic caregiver will learn to recognize when the child is being affected by a trigger, offer immediate support to the child as she undergoes her internal processing, and will assist the child in rethinking the event in the here and now. The therapeutic caregiver helps the child to understand that the abuse was in the past, and that the pain brought on by the trigger is pain brought about inside the child's own mind. Such supportive interactions, occurring over many days and months, will act as a strong opportunity for rebuilding a new sense of self.

Managing Flashbacks

If a child experiences flashbacks or panic attacks within the therapeutic milieu, she will need a combination of reassurance and education. The caregiver can reorient her to the "here and now," encourage her to use all her senses to reestablish contact with the present, and reassure her that the danger is over and that she is not alone. The child will learn that she has available to her a therapeutic guide who is able to assist her in expressing her memories or feelings about the trauma that have been prompted by the flashback. Such therapeutic support offered in the instant that it is needed is the hallmark of the strength of the therapeutic milieu.

Recommended Reading

Bass, E., & Davis, L. (1988). *The courage to heal*. New York: Perennial Library.

Beeler, N. G., Rycus, J. S., & Hughes, R. C. (1990). *The effects of abuse and neglect on child development: A training curriculum*. Washington, DC: Child Welfare League of America.

Briere, J. N. (1992). *Child abuse trauma: Theory and treatment of the lasting effects*. Newbury Park, CA: Sage Publications.

Brohl, K. (1996). *Working with traumatized children: A handbook for healing*. Washington, DC: CWLA Press.

Frierich, W. N. (1991). *Casebook of sexual abuse treatment*. New York: W.W. Norton & Co.

Hindman, J. (1989). *Just before dawn*. Ontario, OR: Alexandria Associates.

James, B. (1989). *Treating traumatized children: New insights and creative interventions*. Lexington, MA: Lexington Books.

Macaskill, C. (1991). *Adopting or fostering a sexually abused child*. London: B.T. Batsford, Ltd.

Mather, C. L., & Debye, K. E. (1994). *How long does it hurt?* San Francisco: Jossey Bass Publishers.

Monahan, C. (1993). *Children and trauma: A parent's guide for helping children heal*. Toronto, Ontario: Maxwell MacMillan.

Rutter, M. (1975). *Helping troubled children*. New York: Plenum Press.

van der Kolk, B. (1995). *Counting the cost*. Video. Nevada City, CA: Cavalcade Productions, Inc.

7 Family Intervention

This last chapter discusses the families of children who have been sexually abused and examines the dynamics of an abusing family in terms of the importance of working with the family, the therapist's reactions and biases, characteristics of the nonabusing parent and the abuser, the marital relationship, and the family as a whole. This discussion also covers the effects of extrafamilial abuse on the child, as well as treatment suggestions for the entire family.

The Need to Work with the Family

It is shortsighted for any therapist responsible for the treatment of sexually abused children to ignore the child's family. Psychologically, the child likely is still a part of that family and may continue to have a relationship with them. Indeed, eventually, either in a planned way or at some time in the future, she may even return to live with them.

Families are often underserviced, however. This may be because abusing families are complex, sometimes overwhelming in the sheer number of needs they present. What has occurred in the family is hard to accept, and society tends to handle the emotional reaction of sexual harm to children by creating "monsters" out of the participants in the abuse.

Unfortunately, our struggles to understand and come to terms with abusing families can get in the way of our ability to help the child we are working with. We forget that we need to deal with the fact that each family member has in some way contributed to the abuse. We may not attend to the fact that each family member (including other children) has a perspective about and experience of the abuse, and that often members of the family are searching for the resources they need to deal with or resolve the abuse.

There may be dynamics in the family that continue to traumatize the child, even though the actual abuse is no longer occurring. The child may feel burdened by opinions she feels family members have of her. She may feel or be made to feel responsible for the family's "destruction." She may feel she has caused family members huge amounts of pain, and she carries around the guilt for this as well as self-blame for the abuse. The child will be subject to these dynamics both in cases of intrafamilial and extrafamilial abuse.

To help the child successfully complete the healing process, the child's case management team must address how the family either supports or continues to harm the child. For example, the myths that exist inside the abusing family need to be dispelled. The case manager should not excuse the abusing behavior or the denial of abuse, but should will work hard at understanding the human pain and need that has led the family to the abuse in the first place and to find the right resources to address that pain.

Reactions and Biases

Often, when a group of people get together to discuss their work with sexually abused children, a pattern begins to emerge. Some will blame the perpetrator, seeing the person as monstrous and fully responsible. Some will blame the inadequate mother, who has failed to protect the child. Some, sadly, blame the child. The truth of the matter is, we tend to pick our "scapegoat" based on who we react to the most and who affects us personally.

Unfortunately, if we fall in the trap of finding someone to blame, we sometimes set up all family members to become intensely loyal to that person and to view us as the "enemy." We inadvertently cause the family to close ranks against us while we are trying to open up the damaging secrets of the family, and this is counterproductive. Knowing more about the profile of the participants may help us to understand why individuals in the family affect us so negatively and help us to avoid this particular trap.

Family Characteristics

Research available on the characteristics of sexually abusing families does not support the notion that there are clearly identifiable individual or family patterns of functioning in families where sexual abuse has taken place. Indeed, research tends to point the other way, that there are few if any global characteristics and that therefore we cannot "predict" who will abuse nor "detect" abuse on the basis of characteristics.

Practitioners working with abusing families in therapy do recognize, however, certain family structures and interaction styles in the families they serve. When these kinds of family dynamics present themselves over and over, practitioners gain additional learning and expertise from repeated experiences. It is therefore fair to say that there are broad similarities in these families, even if they are not clear enough to stand up to scientific investigation. This section looks at some of those broader dynamics.

More often than not, the mother is the nonabusing parent, and for this reason we have chosen the perspective outlined here. The abuser is referred to as the husband; however, this could be the mother's boyfriend or partner.

The Nonabusing Parent

Characteristically, many of the mothers in sexually abusing families have their own histories of trauma in their families of origin. Commonly, as children they experienced a lack of nurturance, verbal and physical abuse, and sexual abuse, either from within or outside of the family.

In the same way that the children we work with continue to repeat the patterns of the past, the mother who has not resolved her own childhood trauma tends to reenact the dynamics of abuse in other relationships. Consciously or unconsciously, she gravitates toward partners who have some of the same characteristics as her nonnurturing or abusive parent, or she replays patterns of reality that reflect her experiences in her own family.

One scenario of how abuse occurs, which we often see, finds the mother struggling as her marital relationship progresses. She finds more and more of her needs are unmet, and she has to work psychologically harder and harder to "survive." While she is preoccupied with herself, there is "room" left for the abuse to happen. The cycle of betrayal is complete when her own child reveals that sexual abuse has occurred. Once again, she has been betrayed by her partner and now also by her child. Sometimes, the mother's investment in the current relationship precludes her ability to respond to the needs of her child. Or, her own unmet needs limit the extent to which she is able to be responsive. Mothers of victims in sexually abusing families might have the following characteristics:

Inability to trust—As a result of a long history of betrayal, the mother may be unable to trust others. Nothing in her life has shown her that relationships can be relied on, so she is likely to be suspicious, hostile, withdrawn, or ambivalent. A major therapeutic issue involves dealing with the mother's inability to trust others, including the therapist.

Impaired self-image—The mother may literally feel "bad." She experiences herself as damaged, undeserving, and a failure. These feelings obstruct her capacity to respond "reasonably" to the events in her child's life.

Feelings of powerlessness—The mother may feel helpless and hopeless, quite unable to affect her world and its events. Like the sexually abused child, she has no positive experience in determining what happens to her.

Immobilization and preoccupation—The mother is preoccupied with other personally overwhelming aspects of her life. She may be experiencing such complaints and symptoms as depression, psychosomatic complaints, etc. Stuck in her own pain, she is unable to summon the ability to respond to meet her child's needs.

Denial—Just as she ignores or denies her own personal feelings of betrayal, the mother's initial reaction to the child's disclosure may be denial that it happened. Acknowledging her child's abuse necessitates confronting her own. She invests enormous amounts of energy into pushing away her awareness of the abusive relationship. As a result, she becomes a "nonverbal participant" in keeping the family secret of abuse.

Failure to establish and enforce boundaries—Most mothers of incest victims have failed in their responsibility to maintain appropriate limits between themselves, their husbands, and their children. This is not to say that mothers must accept responsibility for their husbands' incestuous behavior. The women must, however, acknowledge their own failure to prevent the incestuous behavior by contributing to and permitting the blurring of role boundaries among family members. For the mother, it is sometimes easier to blame the husband entirely and to perceive herself totally as an additional victim, rather than as a responsible adult.

Anger—Mothers may be filled with unacknowledged rage. This anger is expressed and displaced by transferring it from appropriate sources (i.e., the abuser) to inappropriate sources (i.e., the child). Four interrelated sources of anger might include the following:

- Anger with her own family for traumatizing and failing to protect her;
- Anger with her partner for failing to meet her needs and carrying on an abusive relationship with her child;
- Anger, competitiveness, and jealousy toward her child, who has become a rival—the child has been "participating" in a relationship with her partner that was supposed to have been reserved for her; and
- Extreme anger at herself, feeling frustrated, inadequate, and utterly helpless.

The Abuser

While the aforementioned characteristics may be present in the nonabusing family member, the abuser's ability to keep the family functioning around the secret of abuse should not be underestimated. For example, abusers who enter group treatment programs sometimes talk about the dual role they played, one as good husband, the other as abuser. They talk with pride about the excitement they gained from ensuring that the two roles did not collide. Sometimes they brag about how they were able to keep others, particularly their wives, in the dark. This cannot be forgotten as the treatment process unfolds.

Most often the current experience is not the perpetrator's first experience of abuse. Frequently perpetrators of sexual offenses come from abusive families themselves, where they were involved as witness, victim, or forced participant in abuse scenarios of the past. Their families are generally alienated, isolated, and have poor socialization and communication skills. The abuser will not be obviously recognizable. He will not differ significantly from other people in regards to education, occupation, race, religion, intelligence, mental status, or socioeconomic class.

As a result of their backgrounds, sexual abuse perpetrators often develop as "me first" individuals. The individual has poor coping skills, cannot solve problems, has many overwhelming and unmet needs, and has difficulty interacting with his same age peers. Little in his adult life meets his needs or helps him to feel good about himself.

There are two major forms of offending patterns: the fixated offender and the regressed offender. Both kinds of perpetrators have in common their own histories as victims of abuse. Offender patterns and treatment outcomes, however, are quite different.

Fixated offenders usually begin their perpetrating profiles in adolescence. They most clearly derive sexual satisfaction from children, and males are very often their victims. The abuser's sexual preferences and orientation toward children is not likely to be changed. At best, treatment can teach the perpetrator not to act on his impulses.

Regressed offenders commit about 90% of the sexual offenses against children. These offenders have poor coping skills, cannot manage stress well, and in the face of the stresses or family difficulties, seek sexual gratification from their children as a coping strategy. Outcome after treatment in these situations is somewhat more hopeful, as the offender can be helped to refocus his sexual orientation away from children.

Although it is acknowledged that in real life the pattern of events are seldom as neatly arranged, the list on the following page highlights the differences in personal profile and offender behavior of the two types of perpetrators of sexual abuse.

Fixated*	Regressed
1. Primary sexual orientation is toward children.	1. Primary sexual orientation is to age mates.
2. Pedophile interests begin at adolescence or earlier.	2. Pedophile interests emerge in adulthood.
3. No precipitating stressors or subjective episodes of distress occur before episodes of offending.	3. Precipitating stress usually evident.
4. The sexual interest is persistent and behaviors are compulsive.	4. Involvements may be more episodic.
5. Offenses are preplanned, premeditated.	5. Initial offenses may be impulsive, not premeditated.
6. Offender identifies closely with the victim and equalizes his behavior to the level of the child; alternatively, he may adopt a parent-like role with the child.	6. Offender replaces conflicted adult relationships with involvement with the child; in incest situations the offender abandons his parental role.
7. Male victims are primary targets.	7. Female victims are primary targets.
8. Offender has little or no sexual contact with age mates; offender is usually single or in a marriage of "convenience."	8. Sexual contact with the child coexists with sexual contact with age mates; offender is usually married or in a common-law relationship.
9. Usually no history of alcohol or drug abuse.	9. In most cases the offense may be preceded by alcohol or drug abuse.
10. Immature character; poor peer relationships.	10. Offender seems to be living a traditional lifestyle, but peer relationships are underdeveloped.
11. Offense happens because major life issues have not been resolved and are being acted out.	11. Offending is related to a maladaptive attempt to cope with specific life stresses.

*   Adapted with the permission of The Free Press, a division of Simon &
     Schuster, from *Handbook of clinical intervention in sexual abuse* by Suzanne
     M. Sgroi, M.D. © 1982 by Lexington Books.

Marriage Patterns in Abusing Families

Individual differences in abusing families make it impossible to predict or assess abuse by marriage and interactional patterns. Sometimes there are no clear outward indicators to look for. Sometimes it is not the parent, but a sibling, who is the abuser and only some of the family interactional patterns apply. Sometimes the abuser is an extended family member, such as a grandfather, who has also abused the mother in the past. In those instances the continuous indoctrination into a culture of abuse is the most notable feature in the family's functioning. However, once abuse has been detected and treatment begins, often the dynamics listed below become the target for therapeutic intervention.

Passive Dependent Type

In the *passive dependent* relationship, the husband relates to his wife as a dependent child, rather than as a partner. He is reliant on her to fulfill his emotional needs. Wives with dependent husbands report, "He expects me to behave like his mother all the time."

In contrast, the wives tend to be stronger and more self-assertive women. She may have greater capabilities and better developed social skills than he. Dependent husbands seem unable to "make it on their own" without their wives' support. Since these wives often make conscious decisions to turn away from their husbands and seek gratification elsewhere, they in turn become psychologically absent from the rest of the family.

As the mother becomes more independent, self-sufficient, and less attentive to her husband, he turns to his daughter as a substitute companion. The child is then expected to take care of him emotionally. Eventually his emotional dependency on, and intimacy with, his child evolves into a sexual relationship. In essence the child in this scenario has fully taken over the mother's role as companion, sexual partner, and life mate.

If, when entering adolescence, this daughter wants to end the relationship, the offender will experience extreme anxiety. He feels abandoned by the daughter who has become his caregiver. This anxiety may be lessened if there is another child in the family system to replace the older daughter as caregiver and partner. Frequently, once the older sibling becomes aware that a younger sibling is in danger, she will disclose the abuse. The relationship with the sibling, however, is not always a straightforward "rescue," but may be complicated with rivalry issues.

Aggressive-Dominant Type

In this relationship the husband occupies the dominant role in the family. He maintains power by keeping his family financially dependent on him and socially isolated from the outside world. He uses fear and secrecy to maintain command.

As a part of meeting his own needs through dominance, the perpetrator is attracted to a spouse who is insecure or immature. She will have low self-esteem, limited social skills, and act quite passively in her relationship with her husband. He achieves a feeling of well-being, strength, and control in this marital relationship. Wives in these relationships often report that their husbands make them feel "more like a child than a wife."

Because she is helpless and dependent on him, she cannot offer him much emotional support, so he turns to his daughter to fulfill his emotional needs and sexual demands. He considers sexual access to his daughter to be his right as the head of the family.

Psychologically Absent Mothers

One of the characteristics of psychologically absent mothers of abuse victims is that they fail to protect their children or to limit inappropriate behavior between their partners and children. Psychological absence is practically experienced as physical absence. Often the mother is not present for long periods of time and seems to have more of a sibling relationship with her child than a maternal relationship. The child in turn perceives the mother as being relatively impotent and tends to treat her more like a peer than a mother.

As the abusive relationship between the partner and the child progresses, competition between the mother and child becomes greater. The mother manifests this rivalry through anger, while the child struggles with jealousy.

Family Dynamics

It is often extremely valuable to have a good understanding of the typical dynamics of an abusing family. This is, after all, the context in which the child grew up and explains much of what she expects and believes about family relationships.

Sexually abusing families tend to be isolated and closed-off units. What positive, growth-producing energy that exists inside the family is easily shut down or drained away, with little hope of renewal through interaction with the outside world. Such isolation prevents family members from finding healthy ways to adapt to the world.

The most seriously disturbed families are chaotic and bound to one another in such a way that it is difficult for outside observers to see the separation between individuals. Family members have closed ranks against outsiders, an act meant to protect family members but which instead allows abuse to go on without interruption. In broad terms, and with individual differences, the following characteristics are present in most of these families.

Abuse of power—Individuals in power positions abuse their power in order to meet their own needs. They are not concerned about the harm that may result to others. Abuse of power becomes the major way in which the family interacts. Child sexual abuse is always an aggressive act by the perpetrator. A child has been violated and intruded upon, even when force or violence is not used.

Fear of authority—Family members perceive authority as hostile and threatening. Because power is always exploited and misused within the family, members cannot discern appropriate use from inappropriate use of authority. Therefore, they fear that any authority will be destructive to them. Anxiety, suspicion, denial, and hostility result when attempts to avoid authority are unsuccessful.

Isolation—The incestuous family tends to be isolated and withdrawn from society as a whole even if a large extended family exists. Such families have been described as being "without lifelines." The outside world is perceived as being hostile; the family copes by avoiding interaction with "outsiders."

Powerful family members discourage the weaker members from establishing alliances with people outside the family. Parents in incestuous families, especially dominant fathers, may establish themselves as the sole communicator with the outside world. The ability to abuse power increases in proportion to the amount of social isolation experienced by the family. This isolation results in the family being unable to get support, nurturance, and enjoyment from contact with the outside world.

Denial—The family may expend an enormous amount of energy on denial. They must deny the negative aspects of the family's inner workings in order for life to be bearable. Denial is not an effective coping strategy, as it requires increasingly greater amounts of energy to maintain it as time progresses. Constant denial destroys the individual who uses it and impairs the capacity to see things from another person's point of view. Additionally, all of reality becomes distorted by the effort it requires to maintain the denial, so that family members have a difficult time seeing things in "ordinary" ways.

Lack of empathy—Inability to empathize with others is a common characteristic among perpetrators of sexual offenses. The perpetrator seems to be blind to his victim's fear, pain, and needs. He either cannot see the harm that befalls the child or rationalizes what is happening in almost ludicrously positive terms (i.e., "I was a good father, I was teaching her so no one else would hurt her."). If the abuser could empathize with his victim, he could not so easily continue to abuse.

Poor communication patterns—Poor communication within incestuous families tends to be the rule rather than the exception. In a family where lies, secrets, and the misuse of power underlie everything, what is actually said to one another is a means of cover-up and deceit. Real communication, therefore, rarely happens, and family members never communicate needs and ideas openly.

Further, the isolation experienced by the children in the family tends to decrease opportunities for them to practice better communication skills. Times when communication are very important, such as at school or in the therapeutic relationship, become a challenge for the child who does not have a basis for good communication.

Inadequate controls and limit setting—Perpetrators tend to have poor impulse control and fail to set realistic limits on themselves and others. They cannot delay the gratification of their needs and often abuse power in order to ensure that their emotional needs are met.

What is sometimes confounding in these families is that the perpetrator fears his own impulsive tendencies and deals with these powerful feelings by "projecting" them on others. This allows, for instance, a father to permit his teenage child to sleep with him; when inappropriate touching later occurs, he protests that she has misunderstood his attempts to show her his care and concern. He never takes responsibility for allowing her into his bed in the first place and protests that he, not she, was the victim.

When limits are set, they may be harsh and unrealistic. For instance, the father may provide long lectures on the importance of fidelity or modest dressing, all the while he is failing to abide by his own limits by sexually abusing his daughter.

Blurred boundaries—Physical boundaries are ignored whenever a powerful person inappropriately observes or touches a weaker person. The abuse has emotional and role consequences as well. For instance, the fact that the victim daughter is involved with her father in the role of a wife may provide her with a script for acting as a "wife" in all other areas as well—she might cook meals, make discipline decisions, feel she has to protect the younger children, and generally act in the capacity of "parent" in this family. Physical, emotional, and role boundaries have all been blurred.

Extreme emotional deprivation and neediness—Parents in incestuous families are often preoccupied with finding ways of having their own needs met. The families led by such parents develop an interactive style of chaos, confusion, disorganization, and unreliability in relationships. Children within such families struggle to meet their own needs in an environment where there is not enough nurturance to go around. As a result, the child will not have learned how to have her needs met in a healthy way.

Magical expectations—Individuals living in abusing families often do not have the skills to set goals, develop plans, solve problems, or understand the relationship between cause and effect. They observe that others experience good fortune, but because of their inability to connect what other people do with the good things that happen to them, they assume the good thing must be a result of luck, accident, fate, or rescue—in short, some form of "magic."

Family members tend to seek out their own source of magic through selecting relationships or making choices they hope will meet their needs. There is a magical expectation that this time, in this way, by some unknown means or method, their needs will finally be met.

All members of the incestuous family tend to hold these "magical" beliefs. Perhaps the saddest example of this kind of thinking is the hope that the victim holds when she finally discloses. She may have fantasized a magical outcome, and she is devastated when nothing really changes after her disclosure. Indeed, for a time she may feel much, much worse after exposing the secret.

Treatment of Sexually Abusing Families

Families entering therapy for abuse pose a huge challenge. All too often they would rather break up, be perceived as wicked, accept failure, or even die than to go through the process of changing family relationships. The patterns of abuse are so long standing, and the individual neediness of family members so overwhelming, that they hardly ever choose to give up what little they have for what they do not know.

Instead, the child who has been abused often comes into care experiencing the placement as a punishment. She may feel a keen sense of injustice at being the victim, yet she is the one being punished. Her feelings, however justified, hardly ever help the family to move from its well-defended position; she is allowed to be sacrificed because the prospect of change is too frightening to the family.

With this level of resistance, it is easy to see why clinicians seldom have an opportunity to help families heal from the aftermath of sexual abuse. Therapists that do begin the process are not always rewarded with success for their hard work.

Further, sexually abusing families often have multiple problems. These families face difficulty with finances, housing, problem solving, substance abuse, control of affect (the inability to control emotions or to express them in a well-contained way), mental retardation, mental health issues, etc. It is difficult for the therapist not to be distracted by the issue of the hour instead of focusing on the sexual abuse issues; likewise, when those sexual abuse issues have been addressed, the family still suffers through one crisis after another. Occasionally, however, we have an opportunity to meet families with such courage and such commitment that change does occur.

Making the Decision to Attempt Therapy

In the case of resilient children with a supportive, nonabusing parent who acts strongly to protect the child and block the abusive relationship, the issue of reunification never arises. While there will be issues that need to be addressed, as outlined in the stages of treatment to follow, that child and parent can very likely be helped at home, using some of the nonresidential treatment options outlined elsewhere in this book.

In other families, for a host of reasons, the child must be placed in out-of-home care. The kind of family work to be done, the decision to attempt family therapy, and the goals of that therapy, are all important considerations in these instances.

Children who have been severely affected by abuse, and whose circumstances have been complicated by family problems other than the abuse, often come into residential treatment with significant treatment needs. These children require placement in a therapeutic milieu in order to make progress. If the abuser has left the home, the notion of reunification may sometimes be entertained. These cases are among the most difficult to sort through, because case managers can be lulled into believing the abuse is "solved" by the absence of the abuser. Addressing the often convoluted and destructive family relationships that led to the child's vulnerability in the first place, however, is important. Family therapy in these cases would be essential in order to properly examine the viability of reunification.

In some cases the child yearns to return home even though one parent does not believe her and the offender denies the abuse. In these cases, reunification is a discussion that is forced upon the clinical team because the child cannot seem to make progress without a legitimate attempt at working through family relationships. Family therapy in these cases may help the child come to terms with the reality of a family situation that is unlikely to change, and she will then be free to look for a different future.

Finally, there are families we work with who demonstrate a capacity for making change and tackling difficult issues. It is in these cases where reunification of all of the members of the family is sometimes a possibility. In these cases it becomes exceptionally important to have a means of realistically appraising the likelihood of being able to work through all of the issues surrounding the abuse successfully and reestablishing family life on a new footing. Family therapy can be of real assistance in making good decisions.

This section offers a "best case scenario" family treatment strategy as a beginning point for discussion for practitioners grappling with the difficult issue of facilitating family healing. The treatment suggestions presented here assume a certain degree of appropriate family functioning. A functional parent/child bond is an important indicator to look for. In cases where there is some indication of potential improvement in the family, or a willingness on the part of the abusing parent to accept responsibility and make amends, the case for a therapeutic attempt at reunification, or at least for work on strengthening what is left of family relationships, is compelling.

There are, however, other circumstances in which therapeutic intervention will be extremely challenging. Major family dysfunction, such as severe chaos, multiple partners, below-subsistence living standards, or severe substance abuse should be considered major impediments in making the decision to attempt reunification through therapy. A long history of service use without sustained change, or other proof that the capacity for parenting will not likely improve despite assistance, should be seen as contraindicators for a therapy or reunification attempt.

Mother as Abuser

The issue of family therapy services to families where the abuser is the mother is outstandingly complex. The authors have no experience where therapeutic services have been successfully offered in these situations, either to the mother alone or in participation with her partner. In each of the several cases we have been involved with where mothers were the identified perpetrators, denial was a prominent feature. In some of the cases the abusive nature of the relationship continued throughout court-ordered access visits. Even though these visits were carefully monitored, there were elaborate nonverbal communications underway that the children later told us were surreptitious sexual overtures. There is a further area of concern in cases where mothers are identified as the perpetrators. If the mother was not a satisfactory attachment figure, as might be assumed if she

Patricia (7) and Debbie (4) had just finished attending a court-ordered access visit. The volunteer who drove them back to their treatment foster home wasn't alarmed when the two girls covered themselves with a blanket in the back seat. They were just playing.

The next day their treatment foster mother, Marie, was dealing with sexual behavior in the foster home. She asked, "Girls, you haven't played these sexual games for a long time. What made this happen today?"

"Oh, it's not just today, we did sex yesterday, too" piped Debbie.

"Yesterday? Where were you when you were doing it yesterday?"

"In the car with Mr. Driver."

"On the way home from the visit?" Two heads bobbed up and down.

"Boy, what made that happen?"

"Mum."

"I'm sorry, I don't understand. What about mum?"

"She tapped her tooth."

"Let me see if I have this straight. Your mum tapped her tooth and you did sex. And those things go together."

"Yeah! When mum taps her tooth that means 'I want you girls to do sex.' She always used to do that when we were home. If we had company or something, she liked us to do sex. It was a secret. She said it made her blood hot. So she did it in the visit, and we did sex."

"Oh." Marie sat down and took a deep breath. *Oh, Nelly. Why did these therapeutic moments always have to come as such a shock? There's no time to phone the on-call team member for advice on this one! So here I go...* "And when mum taps her tooth, do you want to do sex?"

---

was the abuser, or if the attachment is extremely pathological, and no healthy attachment was made with the father figure, then family therapy will very likely be contraindicated. An opportunity to develop a selective attachment in a secure substitute family is the higher priority in these cases.

For that reason, the family therapy strategies discussed in the remainder of this chapter apply to the most commonly known situation for sexual abuse—males in a position of power over and abusing a female child, usually father and daughter. Any suggestions offered here can be used equally well for treating the family of a male child who has been abused.

Supporting the Abusing Family

Once the case manager has made the decision that a family might benefit from an attempt at reunification through treatment, a treatment team will need to be assembled. Because of the exceptional challenges posed by this form of treatment, and because the risks of mistakenly returning a child to an actively abusing family are so real, the treatment team will need to include many different areas of expertise and points of view.

At a minimum, the team should consist of a case manager whose role it is to advocate for and protect the child, the therapeutic caregiver and supervising worker, a family therapist who works directly with the family, a cotherapist (preferably a man/woman combination) who will sometimes be in the treatment room, and sometimes behind a one-way mirror, and a clinical supervisor with access either to videotaped sessions or live sessions. If the child has an individual or group therapist, that person should be a member of the team as well.

Because the coordination of a team this size poses challenges, every member of the team will be required to check and double-check safety issues, problem solve, and develop strategies that will be effective as layer after layer of the family's defense structure is uncovered. It is never recommended that a single therapist attempt this process, and it should certainly never be attempted without a child-focused advocate, who is in the position of making the final reunification decision.

Stages of Treatment

The following 12 steps are phases of treatment that are essential to a successful reunification of the entire family, including the abusing parent. The team may make adjustments to the sequence depending on who the abuser is and who is to be reunited. However, most of the steps apply to all reunification scenarios, to one degree or another.

Each stage must be planned carefully, beginning with an assessment of the family's needs, strengths, and risks, followed by a strategy to address those areas. The goal is to work through each family member's individual issues, each subsystem relationship, the parenting issues that emerge, and role and structural problems that become evident. Finally, the family must accept responsibility.

The stages of treatment are listed in sequential order; that is, one must be well in hand, or in some cases even completed, before the next can begin. The decision to reunify is contingent on successful working through of all of the stages.

1. **Blocking the abusive relationship.** The first therapeutic step for any incestuous family is making sure the incest stops. When the nonoffending parent believes the victim, and that parent is willing to protect the child, then the offender can be removed from the family home; if not, then the child must be placed in out-of-home care.

2. **Helping the child overcome the individual impact of abuse.** The child will need to address role confusion, identity issues, self-esteem problems, ambivalence, mistrust, guilt, and behavioral difficulties, as has already been discussed in this handbook. Without sufficient support and progress in these areas, the victim of abuse will be far too vulnerable to the destructive patterns of the family to even attempt family intervention.

3. **Taking full responsibility.** For any further family reunification work that includes the offender to take place, the abuser must admit to the abuse and take full responsibility for it—he and only he caused the abuse to happen. Later it is possible to look at the interrelationships and tensions that contributed to the abuse, but at this stage a "no excuses" stance is needed.

   This is the stage where many cases become "stuck." The parent has so much to lose by admitting to the abuse. He feels so threatened at the idea of accepting responsibility that he would rather be jailed or even commit suicide than admit the abuse occurred.

   In some programs a court-ordered requirement for therapy acts as an alternative to jail. The offender has the option of admitting abuse took place and getting help, or going to jail. If he "runs away" from therapy once it begins, jail is the consequence. The situations where there is a strong legal requirement to come to therapy are those where the highest degree of success is experienced.

4. **Identifying the offender's support needs**. The offender may be angry at the spouse for failing to meet his needs. He may be having trouble recognizing his angry feelings and may have extremely poor stress and anger management skills. Since his daughter provided for him some level of support, he will need to find other ways of feeling accepted and cared for. Other treatment issues for the offender may involve learning impulse control, emotional regulation, and attending to alcohol or drug dependency (often present in incest cases as a means of lowering inhibitions to the abuse or providing a psychological "excuse" as in, "I was drunk."). Attempts to "run away" from treatment in the form of a suicide attempt are a real problem that may well confront the therapeutic team.

5. **Attending to the needs of the mother**. The mother may feel she needs to be "taken care of." She may lack social skills or be unassertive. She may carry around anger about the role she was forced to play in the marriage, either as "mother" to a dependent husband or "child" to a dominant husband. Frequently these mothers feel intense depression that will need to be addressed as well. All of these needs should be addressed prior to the next major treatment step.

6. **Admitting maternal responsibility in the abuse**. The mother will need to come to terms with the fact that she failed to protect her child from abuse. She will have to confront the fact that she may have overlooked clues, denied reality, or sacrificed her daughter in order to avoid or lessen conflict in her family. Finally, she must find the strength to recognize that her daughter has become her husband's partner and that in some way she had a role in losing him.

7. **Taking joint and equal responsibility as parents for failing to parent adequately**. This is the first step in restructuring the family that has had no boundaries. The parents must accept their rightful role as parents of the child, with all of the responsibili-

ties that come with the role. They must recognize that the child belongs in the "child position" in the family. Treatment then focuses on the skills and strategies necessary to parent effectively.

8. **Working on the mother-daughter relationship**. It is often felt that this part of the family work is the least "loaded" emotionally. Therapists are therefore shocked to discover the fierce competition that emerges between mother and daughter. The mother has to accept that in some ways she set the child up to take her role. Sometimes the child, especially in adolescence, is openly triumphant over the mother, having taken her role, her power, and her intimacy.

   Active battles for alignment also occur—will the mother stay with the husband and align against the daughter or align with the daughter against the husband? These are extremely stressful times for such fragile and needy individuals.

   The mother-daughter relationship cannot be resolved until the daughter comes to terms with her disappointment with her mother as a mother, and the mother comes to terms with her daughter's intimacy with the father.

9. **Working on the marital relationship**. At the early stages the mother may threaten to leave the husband. Later the husband and wife may align against the daughter. The mother may feel frightened by the depth of her husband's despair—his suicidal threats or his clear inability to function—and feel compelled to come to the rescue. Later the real underlying marital conflicts come out in the open. The parents begin to look at the role each had to play in the incest.

   In a family where communication is so poor, and where family members are able to deny so well that they keep secrets even from themselves, the stresses of opening up the pain and anger can be overwhelming. Stress-related physical disorders (i.e., anxiety attacks, somatic complaints, or even heart attacks) can be the result of the strain. Significant courage, support, and/or leverage is needed for the family to keep going at this stage.

   Both parents are working toward being able to see themselves as equally responsible. Each becomes aware of how they fed into the incest. The partners are better able to understand each others' needs and have their own needs met appropriately. When they have achieved these stages and established communication founded on a new set of "rules," it may be time to introduce the father-daughter dyad.

10. **Working on the father-daughter relationship**. Once all of the other key relationship issues have been resolved, it becomes possible for victim and perpetrator to reassess their relationship. The perpetrator must continue to accept full responsibility, and the treatment team supports his apology to his daughter. The secrecy and overly close relationship between father and daughter may explode into open hostility on the part of the daughter toward the father.

    To reunite as a family, the daughter must work through her anger, give up her power, and allow herself to take her role as a child in the family. The perpetrator must give up his pathological method of having his needs met through the abuse of power and must convince his daughter that it is safe for her to take her role as a daughter in the family.

    Sometimes only partial solutions can be found. Some sense of connectedness for the victim with family members may be enough for her in her own personal healing process. Abandoning the fantasy father of her dreams, accepting the reality of who the father is, and learning to be no longer controlled by him would also be good outcomes.

11. **Working on the family structure**. Assuming all of the above can be accomplished, the final stage is to help the family make the deep and lasting structural changes necessary for the abuse not to occur again. "Enough" distance needs to be created between parents and children and "enough" closeness between parents. The family will clarify roles, and the treatment team will help parents learn appropriate strategies for parenting and problem solving. Working together, the team and the family will address communication issues and actively target the family's self-imposed isolation. Finally, family sessions can focus on helping family members come to understand more about one another, including likes, dislikes, and expectations of one another.

12. **Reunification**. If, and only if, all of the above steps have been resolved can the family fully reunite with any degree of safety. It is clear that not all families will be able to tolerate the intensity of the work required to make full reunification a possibility. Those that make it deserve every credit for the incredible courage it required to do the work.

The Alternative of Good-Enough Relationships

Sometimes reunification is not an option. However, children need to sort through their relationships with the significant individuals in their lives. Family work, while not aimed at reunification, can aim for resolution.

The clinical reasons for working toward the best relationships possible are numerous. Some of the most compelling reasons are listed below:

- Children need to develop a realistic understanding of the strengths, weaknesses, motivations, and potential of their family members. Without such realism, children can become "stuck" in fantasies about a well-functioning family that has moved on without them, or "stuck" in a self-perception of being the responsible, wrong child. Personal healing can be significantly compromised in children where family relationships are not put to rest.

- Children who feel as if they are "drifting" in out-of-home care can feel a great deal more empowered if they perceive that an active attempt is being made to sort through family issues. Even though the outcome might not be a confession on the abuser's part, and declaration of support by the nonoffending parent, the child may find comfort in knowing that everything possible was tried.

- Abused and traumatized children have already lost a great deal. It would be unfair not to work toward a future where there is some sense of belonging to an extended family, even if that belonging is untraditionally organized. There is an obligation to preserve as much about what was positive about the past as possible, whether that be only in the child's mind, or in the actual relationships.

When the child's family is available for intervention, it makes good clinical sense to work as far through the reunification steps as possible, adjusting the clinical goals along the way. Reasonable communication, an absence of overt harm between family members, and a realistic understanding of how the abuse happened, and what can reasonably be expected from family members, can be good alternatives to reunification.

Extrafamilial Abuse

In these situations the perpetrator is not the primary caregiving figure, but is highly likely to be known to the family. In a substantial proportion of cases, the victim's parent will have permitted the perpetrator to have access to the child. For instance, he may have been a visitor to the home or have been asked to baby-sit. Treatment in this instance relates to helping the family understand the contribution it has made to the victimization and helping the child and family overcome the impact.

The critical family issue is usually a failure to protect the child. This often involves poor supervision or an inappropriate choice of caregiver. Treatment involves a comprehensive child management strategy, a parenting/peer support group, and specific training in how to select baby-sitters. The exception is if the abuse was perpetrated by someone with an important family role, such as the mother's boyfriend. In those instances treatment would be more similar to that for intrafamilial abuse.

Victim support issues center more around helping the family not to view the child as being "damaged" by her too-early introduction to sexuality. Family sessions that clear the air and bring any sibling or parent concerns about the victim out into the open will be helpful. The therapist models an appropriate tone of concern for, but acceptance and validation of, the child victim.

M arnie was 13 when she came into the treatment foster home.

This was her second foster home. The first had broken down when Marnie's behavior began to deteriorate. She was angry, noncompliant, seductive, and a constant source of irritation to her former foster family.

The beginning of Marnie's deterioration could be traced back to a criminal court case. Marnie had alleged sexual abuse perpetrated by her stepfather. He denied everything, and Marnie's mother chose to believe him. However, the police laid charges, and Marnie was hopeful that, finally, he would admit the abuse and her mother would stand by her.

Unfortunately, Marnie made a terrible witness in criminal court. Her cognitive delays, memory lapses, lack of logical thought, confusion, and inaccurate memories, all so understandable as the after effects of the abuse experience, meant that her testimony was not reliable. Her stepfather was found "not guilty." Instead of her dream resolution, Marnie now had to face a father who openly gloated and a mother who said, "Admit it now, you lied. Come home."

The sense of complete failure, and perception of betrayal by her parent, the court, and the child protection system, served only to traumatize Marnie once again. Whatever coping ability she had was completely eroded.

During her placement at the treatment foster home, Marnie struggled. It would all be so much easier if she recanted and went home. However, with support, she was able to come to terms with what had happened to her, understood the significance of it, and, finally, reached the point where she was not prepared to sacrifice her own well-being in order to accommodate her family's version of truth.

While still symptom ridden and often crippled by fears and memories, she was beginning to enter the stage where she needed to establish a goal for herself in order to make sense of her past and to re-create her future. Marnie could not let go of the idea that, if she had not failed in court, her father would have confessed and her mother would have believed her.

Her desire to go home, and to somehow magically return to a state where her mother loved her and she "belonged," became overwhelming. She refused to work on anything else other than getting home. Her parents expressed the same desire. The sooner Marnie returned home, the sooner the awful nightmare would be over. They agreed to come into family sessions in order to see what could be done about getting Marnie home.

The treatment team convened and selected two therapists, a man and a woman. A great deal of effort went into establishing how to approach the first session. We could not seriously entertain the notion of reunification unless Marnie's stepfather was prepared to admit the abuse had taken place. However, if we did not accept the family's denial of the abuse at face value, it would likely mean losing the family early in the process. Marnie needed an opportunity to believe she had done everything within her power to resolve her family situation. It would be important for her to leave the family therapy process "guilt free." The team established a way of talking about the abuse that everyone could agree to: "Someone in the family is lying." This allowed us to have extensive discussions about the individual impacts of the abuse for all family members, without being stumped by denials. We explored what needed to be resolved before reunification and worked hard to establish a climate where the family's agreed-upon solution, whatever it might be, was the goal we were working toward.

Having bypassed the crucial step of taking responsibility, we began to work on the attention needs of all of the family members. Father complained that his wife was not "motherly" enough. She had left him in charge of discipline too much, and he needed her as a partner. Mother talked about her own history as a victim of abuse, and her fear that once she started to discipline, she would become harsh and abusive. She felt too weak, she said. We reframed it as a worry that she might be too strong. Within the sessions themselves she started to parent actively. Marnie, who had been acting as parent in her mother's stead, was relegated to a "kid position" in the family.

For weeks the parents explored the roles, parenting styles and structures of the family, and the marital relationship. The "someone is lying" framework provided a way to talk about what would need to be changed if the family were to reunite, so the same problems would not reoccur. The discussion went on in detail, despite the lack of admission of responsibility.

Eventually, though, we had worked around the problem long enough, and the family began to move on resolving "who is lying." It began when the father asked if anything legal would happen if "someone" admitted to the lie. This required the protection agency to make a courageous decision. It was more important, they felt, for Marnie to have her admission than for a criminal proceeding to occur. The agency told the family that there was nothing to be gained by criminal charges. The family kept coming back, week after week, working around the problem.

Finally one week Marnie's mother came in to the session and said "I can't stand this anymore. Someone in my family is lying, and I don't know who it is, and it's killing me!" The stepfather hid behind his ball cap. Marnie reached out to her mother. They sat together in this state, the insurmountable problem before them and between them. The therapists reflected on how difficult that must be for them all, and wondered whether anyone would ever have the courage to take the next step.

That night Marnie's stepfather had a heart attack. While it was never openly stated, it was clear to all that he had tried to reach for courage, and found it was too much. He recovered, but the family work could not continue.

Marnie now proved herself to have the most courage of all. She was the victim, not the abuser, she said. She would not "take it back" even to save her stepfather's life. If this meant she could not go home, so be it.

Mother stated overtly that she was not prepared to have her husband die in order to solve the dilemma. Mother did one more thing, the clinical interpretation of which intrigued the therapists. She went to see a psychic, who "read" that her husband had hurt her daughter. On the audiotape Mother expressed her deep upset and remorse that such a thing "might" have happened. She gave the tape to Marnie.

It was enough. Marnie was able to move on to a new future, one she created for herself. She did not visit her family again, although she exchanged letters with her siblings. She spoke to her mother only rarely, and to her stepfather not at all. Marnie asked for group and individual therapy and, in combination with the support of the milieu, began to grow as if the weight of the world had been lifted from her.

On the night of her high school graduation, Marnie's mother slipped quietly into the front row. She was there to see her daughter win several major awards, including Student of the Year and a scholarship for college. She never spoke to Marnie and left as quietly as she had come. She had done the best she could. It was enough to allow her daughter to break free. It was not the usual outcome for intensive family therapy, but it was a satisfying one.

Recommended Reading

Berg, I. K. (1991) *Family based services: A solution focused approach.* Milwaukee, WI: BFTC Press.

Furniss, T. (1983). Family process in the treatment of intrafamilial child sexual abuse. *Social Casework, 64,* 263–279.

Gelles, R. J., & Strauss, M. A. (1988). *Intimate violence: The causes and consequences of abuse in the American family.* New York: Simon and Schuster.

Horowitz, A. N. (1983) Guidelines for treating father daughter incest. *Social Casework, 64,* 515–524

Kagan, R., & Schlosberg, S. (1989) *Families in perpetual crisis.* New York: W. W. Norton & Co.

Sgroi, S. (1982). *Handbook of clinical intervention in child sexual abuse.* Lexington, MA: Lexington Books.

Smith, D. W., & Saunders, B. E. (1995). Personality characteristics of father/perpetrators and non-offending mothers in incest families: Individual and dyadic analysis. *Child Abuse and Neglect, 19,* 607–617.

Steinhauer, P. D. (1993). *The least detrimental alternative: A systematic guide to case planning and decision making for children in care.* Toronto, Ontario: University of Toronto Press.

Afterword: Reflections from the Sanctuary

Throughout this book you have met the children with whom we work. Their stories are heartbreaking, sometimes shocking. But the children's courage, their abilities, and their endless capacity for growth and change are what, for us, stand out in the long run. Because of their potential and their receptiveness to what we were trying to do, we as the caregiver team felt a deep obligation to do this work well.

It was not easy to learn to work with a severely traumatized child population in a way that would respect their experiences and address their true needs. Learning to look beyond behavior and to find a way of talking to the children that would unleash their own capacity for healing was harder than any of us ever imagined.

You have met the treatment team—caregivers, supervising support workers, and others—briefly in the case examples throughout the book. They are real people, and the conversations you have read really happened. What follows are "notes from the sanctuary," the thoughts and comments of the staff members and foster parents who first took the journey into learning to treat the aftermath of sexual abuse in the professional foster care environment.

From the Child Care Consultants

These are the reflections of the social workers and child and youth care workers who coordinate the case planning and provide weekly supervision to the treatment homes. In their hands lies the responsibility of converting theory into practical application for use on individual cases in the treatment foster homes under their supervision.

139

How many courses did you take on sexual abuse while you were being trained? Nothing I took prepared me for the kind of thoughtfulness, thoroughness, and analytical approach that is needed in these cases.

The hardest part was letting go of the past ways you had of treating kids, of what you were good at; when I let it go it opened up a whole new framework that I could use. However, I needed the whole framework before the bits and pieces started to make sense.

Behavior was no longer something to change but to understand; by modifying behavior I was modifying how the child was speaking. In this style you help the child take responsibility for the communication, rather than the behavior. The treatment parent's job is as much to explore and muse ("I wonder if ...") as it is to correct, set limits, teach.

Looking beyond the immediate milieu for an explanation of a particular set of behaviors leads to different management choices than you might have thought of by looking only inside the daily living environment. Sometimes the thing that is *right* to do in order to get to the big picture seems like the opposite of what you *should* do.

Let me give you an example. Mandy peed on the carpet in her room, and Deanna just lost it. She really disciplined Mandy hard for her behavior. So Mandy got some paper cups, peed in them, and left them all lined up on the carpet. It is as if she was saying, "All right, I'll follow your darned rules about the carpet, but I still have something to say!" Deanna got the message the second time and was able to go in talk about what was on Mandy's mind. *Then* they talked about a better way of letting someone know what the problem is other than peeing on the carpet.

The treatment parents really had to trust us at first. It wasn't always logical, and sometimes the behaviors increased while we struggled to understand what was being communicated. However, once we were on the right track the child signaled us by giving up the behavior.

Supervision sessions with the treatment parents become a modeling of technique. The better *I* became at a nondirective, musing style, the more quickly the treatment parents learned it.

I felt like I was swinging all over the place. It was important for me to remember that it was the concepts that were swinging, not the daily care in the milieu. The milieu had to stay rock solid.

The adult has to take responsibility for missing the message, rather than the child for misbehaving. It can be a heavy burden, taking ownership for listening more closely. This is not broad-stroke treatment. It is extremely precise, and one moment can feel like it means everything.

You have to get comfortable with not having the answers, with knowing "nothing." This is closer to the real truth for me anyway, and it freed me up from feeling punitive, angry, and manipulated by the kids. I learned to come at the problem with a question instead of a solution.

To teach the techniques to the treatment parents, we used the same reflective musing technique. Sometimes they found it really frustrating. One in particular used to say, "Just give me the answer!" Finally we had to do guided exercises. I asked her to talk to me about when I was a little boy in the hospital and "muse" about what that would have been like for me. Letting go of the idea that she was supposed to already have the answer to supply me with was a little like dangling over the edge of a cliff for her; would you let go? But once she understood that the answers were already inside me, and that this was an exercise in listening and imagining, she managed to put away her black-and-white thinking. She became an explorer.

From the Doctors

The doctors are the program's extended clinical team, the psychologists, psychiatrists, and therapists who act as the consultant teachers to our work. Here are some of their reflections as they watched the team struggle with learning a new approach.

Don't allow your attention to be diverted from the importance of safety. You may be fooled into thinking that you have created an emotional sanctuary long before you really have.

Once you have the "story," do not imagine that the child has envisaged a new way to behave. That work comes only after a good period of mourning.

I wonder what that would be like if you looked at it from the child's perspective?

For some children the right thing to do is to let them repress and get on with their lives. You do not have to do uncovering work in every case.

These are very lucky children.

From the Parent Therapists

Treatment parents, milieu-based therapists, therapeutic foster parents. Our name for them is Parent Therapists. At long last, a word from the people who care for these children every day, and who have taught us that it *is* possible to live with your therapist if he or she is very good at what they do. You met them in the cases. Here are their thoughts on what this work is like. You'll notice that the thoughts are as varying as the personalities that are expressing them.

This is slow work, very, very slow. You don't know how hard it is until you have your nose right in it.

We're on their schedule, not they on ours.

You need to know the kids really well before you start this work. You need to know their moods, their signs, when to push and when not to push.

It's hard to feel confident in this work. Usually you feel like you don't know enough, inadequate.

Sometimes when you start a therapeutic conversation with a kid, you get lost in it.

It can be scary work. You worry you will say the wrong thing and shut it down for good. It's such a relief when the kid comes back to try again.

This is one time when not knowing the answers actually helps. The kids are very patient about explaining it to you. Be a "dumb blonde!"

Never, ever say "I know how you feel." You don't. Even imagining how they feel is overwhelming. This is true even if you've been abused yourself.

Therapeutic conversations always seem to happen just when the dog barfs on the floor or something! It's never a good time!

Formal sit-down times never worked for my kid. She did better when she was just lying on the bed, yapping.

My two girls really enjoyed the more structured formal counseling times, where we used the therapeutic stories and art. The rest of the time they were "just kids" and it was great for them.

You cannot, honestly, win them all. Don't get discouraged.

I'm still getting over the fact that Jen would not let me go any further. She ended it and discharged herself before she had anywhere near finished what she needed to do.

What helps most? Support! To know you're not alone. To have your clinical team just a phone call away. To have someone to talk about it with, every single week. To know there is a whole team of thinkers backing you up. If something doesn't work, all of us take responsibility, not just me.

Yes, and to be a part of a group of Parent Therapists. To hear others have made the same mistake and survived. To laugh about it. A chance to talk about what it's like with people who actually know what you're talking about.

From the Management

When we first began I thought we were taking a huge gamble. We were moving completely away from a traditional, behavioral/cognitive approach and moving into something that, at times, looked an awful lot like psychotherapy. We traveled with the help of expert advice, but it took a great deal of courage in leadership nonetheless. Now, in hindsight, I wonder what all the fuss was about. Once the conversion was made, it was as natural as breathing. I can't imagine working any other way, now.

From a Child

When you are lucky enough to have a child work all the way through the healing stages and graduate from your setting, you have the best education of all. These young adults are remarkably aware of what went on in the milieu and can give you the kind of insightful evaluation of how you did, which is at once exhilarating and earth shattering.

When we first started, none of our children were reaching this point. Now, almost all of them do. But Marnie was the first, our most powerful, articulate teacher. Here is Marnie's message.

> Be there. Twenty-four hours a day, seven days a week. I never know when it will hit, and it could be any time. I will throw anything at you during those times, words, things, whatever. Be there with me.
>
> Give me support and loving care, but only to a point. Don't get too close to me, like family, or I won't be able to do the work with you. I need you to feel like a little bit of a stranger in order to open up safely.
>
> Near the end, when I was finishing, it started to get hard. She (my Parent Therapist) started to say, "We're going to do this or do that" but then we never did. I felt she was getting too attached to me, that she felt if I finished the work I would leave. I did finish and I did leave. Now our relationship is very different. We're more like "equals." But we're closer than ever.

Appendix A
Outline for Three-Day Training

Day One

9:30 A.M.   **Introduction, housekeeping**

9:45 A.M.   **History of Treatment Foster Care's interest in the topic**
* Development of TFC
* Research findings
* Child population
* Role of clinical team
* Development and use of the handbook

10:00 A.M.   **Understanding the impact of abuse from the child's perspective**
* What is sexual abuse?
* What are the psychological, behavioral, and developmental impacts of abuse?
* What does abuse look like from the child's point of view? How can we find out?

Noon   **Lunch**

1:00 P.M.   **Treating abused children**
* What is treatment?
* What should we do for children who have been sexually abused? What are our goals?
* What methods of treatment are available? What roles does the method play in meeting the goals?
* How do I select the kind of treatment my child needs?

3:30 P.M.   **Review of the day, setting priorities for Day Two**

Day Two

9:30 A.M.   **Housekeeping, review, questions**

10:00 A.M.   **Building a safe milieu**
- What is a "milieu"?
- How should it be organized for these children?
- What works? What doesn't work?
- What are the changing roles of the support team in this work? (i.e., therapists, group workers)

Noon   **Lunch**

1:00 P.M.   **Stages of healing**
- What are the stages of healing that a child travels through?
- The prestory, story, poststory stages
- What issues are likely to come up in foster care? How do I deal with them?

3:00 P.M.   **Messages from the children**

3:30 P.M.   **What is one thing I will change?**

Day Three

9:30 A.M.   **Housekeeping**

9:45 A.M.   **Helping children deal with their families**
- What do we know about the abusers?
- What do we know about the nonoffending parents?
- How do we think children view their families?

What should we do for them?
- What are the blocks and challenges to treatment?
- What are the typical stages of treatment for abusing families (intrafamilial, extrafamilial)?
- How will children perceive what we do for them? How will their perceptions affect the milieu?
- Can we reunify?
- What are the implications for practice?

(This half-day's discussion should pull as much from the agency's in-house expertise as from the trainer. The goal is to leave the discussion "ongoing" in the agency.)

11:30 A.M.   **What is one thing I will change?**

Appendix B
Effects of Abuse on Child Development

INFANTS AND TODDLERS (BIRTH TO 3 YEARS)

Normal Development	Results of Abuse
Physical	
Birth–One: Develops ability to control own muscles.	Delays in both gross and fine motor skills, muscles can be poorly developed if neglect or physical abuse is also present.
One–Two: Develops balance, coordination, and stability.	Sleep problems, apparent fear around sleep time. Problems with toilet training. Internal damage, such as pain, inflammation, bruising, bleeding, scarring, sexually transmitted diseases.
Two–Three: Develops increased strength and coordination, can meet challenges in the environment (bikes, stairs, playground equipment, crayons, etc.), ready to be toilet trained.	Intense sexualized feelings, leading to excessive masturbation.
Cognitive	
Birth–One: Beginning to be alert and aware, can recognize significant people. Interested in looking, listening, touching. Can remember objects even if they are hidden (object permanence).	Apathy, listlessness, immobile.
One–Two: Understands that objects have names, that the names mean something (symbolic thought), and learns to use the names.	Delay of speech, including loss of already developed speech in extreme cases. Does not explore environment or manipulate objects, lacks curiosity.
Two–Three: Able to speak more clearly, use words to communicate with others.	Does not master basic ideas, such as object permanence or basic skills in problem-solving, may appear to be developmentally delayed if severely neglected as well as sexually abused.
Social/Emotional	
Birth–One: Attaches to caregiver, then learns to trust the caregiver.	Failure to form attachments and trust relationships, lack of ability to pick out significant people.
One–Two: Affectionate and trusting relationships develop with people other than the primary caregiver. Can play simple games.	Does not appear to notice or respond to separation from parent, may not show stranger anxiety.
Two–Three: Enjoys playing "beside" other children. Likes to do things by herself. Understands the idea of "good" and bad."	Inability to relate with other children, may touch others inappropriately, shows adult knowledge of sexual behavior.
	Cautious, watchful, on guard, "frozen," perception of self as a bad child, fearful, anxious.
	Avoids or is alarmed by visual or tactile reminders of the abuse (triggers).

PRESCHOOL (3 TO 5 YEARS)

Normal Development	Results of Abuse
Physical	
Most gross motor skills have been developed, now being practiced. Enjoys new physical challenges.	Motor skills may be delayed or absent. Poor muscle tone, poor motor coordination, lack of strength if neglect, confinement, or understimulation were part of the abuse.
	Sleep problems, fearfulness, nightmares and night terrors, fear of being alone and going to sleep).
	Psychosomatic complaints (aches and pains that have no physical basis).
Cognitive	
Language develops well, words are used in correct order, and vocabulary increases rapidly, can communicate in words.	Speech may be absent, delayed, or hard to understand.
Ideas are concrete and center around herself. Cannot yet follow a step-by-step approach to solving problems, but can draw conclusions based on little information. At this age children have many fantasies, and their facts and fantasies are often mixed together.	Receptive language (ability to understand what is being said) may be far better than expressive language (the ability to express self in words). Can eventually lead to a learning disability.
Poor understanding of cause and effect.	May have an unusually short attention span, not be interested in things in her surroundings, have trouble concentrating.
Reasoning may not make sense to us, but makes perfect sense to the child. When adult points out flaws, child stubbornly clings to her version.	Thinking skills may present as those of a younger child. Tries to make sense of the traumatic experience. When the child cannot understand an event, may make up a magical explanation for it.
	Sees images of unpleasant memories of the traumatic events. These images pop into the child's mind against her will, and she is unable to talk about them.
Social/Emotional	
Has relationships with adults outside of the family. Can interact and play cooperatively with peers.	Play shows confusion about the events that have injured or shocked the child. Other children might also be enlisted to "play out" the trauma. May include aggression, sexualized touching of others.
Understands, explores, and pretends about "social roles" (i.e., this is what mommy does, or I'm a fireman).	
Learns the concept of right and wrong, can judge her own behavior in relation to others, which affects her sense of self.	Excessively fearful, anxious, easily upset, or apathetic, loss of interest in activities
Experiences guilt when she has behaved badly.	
Able to try new things, likes to take charge, and can take initiative in activities. No longer dependent.	

SCHOOL AGE (6 TO 12)

Normal Development	Results of Abuse

Physical

Normal Development	Results of Abuse
Practices, refines, and masters complex gross and fine motor skills.	Can experience toileting accidents (wetting pants, soiling).
The child is energetic, active, "always on the go."	Also see previous stages.
Boys tend to be more "rough and tumble," girls more adept at fine motor skills, probably because of what they are encouraged to do by adult caregivers (socialization).	
Experiences some discomfort or embarrassment about sexual topics, urges, and own development.	

Cognitive

Normal Development	Results of Abuse
Instead of being magical and self-centered, the child is now capable of thinking that is more logical and rational.	"Intrusions" of unwanted thoughts and images and memories of the trauma. These images disrupt concentration and create anxiety.
The child is now capable of observing and correctly understanding how relationships, actions, objects, etc., work. She can develop ideas about how to interact with things to make them work out well (concrete operational thought).	Performance at school can be affected because of inability to concentrate.

Ordinary life events (seasons, special occasions, etc.) have become strongly associated with and can bring on memories of the abuse. Perceptions of these events or seasons have been distorted by the abuse. |
| The child is less self-centered, more able to see other people's points of view and to act on those perceptions. | The child's memories of the traumatic events have been affected and changed by the child's fears or wishes about the event. The length of the event can seem either longer or shorter than it actually was, which can upset the child's sense of time. |

Social/Emotional

Normal Development	Results of Abuse
Relationships outside of the immediate family take on importance to the child. She enjoys participating in her peer groups.	Anxiety, fearfulness, fear of traumatic event re-occurring. Fears and mistrusts all adults. Intensity of own feelings are frightening.
The child imitates, learns, and adopts the behaviors of those around her. Being like others and fitting in takes on importance for the first time.	Secretive reenactment or playing out of the traumatic event.

May be able to talk about the sexual abuse. Sometimes repeatedly talks about the traumatic event, seemingly without getting any relief in the telling. |
The child understands rules, why they exist, and what happens if they are not adhered to. She is interested and concerned with following rules.	
The child is hard-working, has goals and a purpose, and can organize her activities to meet goals.	Either withdrawn and quiet or excessively aggressive and testing rules and limitations.
She is becoming more aware of herself as an individual, and the child's self-esteem is affected by how she sees herself (self-perception).	Engages in behaviors that cannot be mistaken as anything else but sexual aggression or intrusiveness (simulated or actual intercourse, fondling, etc.) Relates to adults in a sexual way.

ADOLESCENCE (13+)

Normal Development	Results of Abuse
Physical	
As the body matures into adulthood, hormones cause changes. Includes fast physical growth and a new physical maturity. This also includes development of the sexual organs.	Accident prone.
	Problems with sleeping.
The changes in the body need getting used to. Some of the changes mean the child will need to behave differently (i.e., physically maturing girl will feel less comfortable with touch football).	Eating disorders, such as bulimia or anorexia. See also previous stages.
The body becomes ready for sexual interaction and is able to reproduce.	

Cognitive	
Thinking has become almost adult in its complexity. Adolescents can develop an idea, look at its various points of view, and logically analyze the idea (thinking hypothetically).	The memories and images of the trauma become acute and pierce into the child's day-to-day living. The child is extremely aware of these images and distressed by them.
The adolescent can, for the first time, think about the process of thinking in an abstract way, especially in mid- and late adolescence.	"Flashback" episodes (sudden memories of the traumatizing event) become more frequent and have more negative impact.
Insight is developed. Can solve problems by thinking about them in detail, working out complex solutions, and evaluate those solutions.	

Social/Emotional	
Peers are more important than family relationships.	Teen feels shame, guilt, humiliation. The inner turmoil (tension) is managed through unhelpful tension reducers (running, withdrawal, sexual acting out, etc.)
The values and ideals of the peer group will be more important to the teen than the parents' ideas in terms of guiding their behavior.	
Peer acceptance is important to self-esteem. Feeling "different" is unacceptable.	Wish for revenge or action to "put things right." Vulnerable to depression, pessimism, fear of growing up.
First interest in the opposite sex, leading to interest in sex itself. Some teens will experiment with sex.	Clings to remaining in the protection of a family, even if the family is negative.
Moods swing; teens are quite reactive to emotional stress.	Child wants to escape the horror of the trauma and mistakenly believes that adult behavior (i.e., early marriage, childbirth, dropping out of school, change from peer to adult relationships) will somehow take her away from having to work out the impact of the abuse.

Appendix C
Milieu-Based Therapeutic Tasks

Stage of Growth

Prestory	Story	Poststory
Child has not yet told her story.	Child begins to struggle with the reality and pain of the abuse experience. She remembers and talks about abuse and explores pains, fears, and ambivalences about the relationship with the abuser and significant others.	Child continues to work on resolving past relationships, this time with a focus of becoming personally empowered. Child begins to be able to entertain the notion of a positive future and take positive steps toward it.
Clues to the child's story are being communicated through behavior and social cues.		
Child perceives herself as unsafe, despite efforts to help her feel safe. Child has no experience that caregivers can be nonabusive.	Child begins to understand that there is a connection between feelings, behaviors, and consequences. She understands her behavior has a meaning that can be talked about.	Child ceases being a "victim" of sexual abuse, begins to work on becoming a survivor.
Child not yet ready to trust adults or talk about what has happened.		Termination of the intense therapeutic relationship begins at the end of this stage.
	Child begins slowly to risk openness and allows herself to confront painful memories. Trauma assessment can occur.	

Therapeutic Objectives

Prestory	Story	Poststory
Provide a safe container/ emotional sanctuary:	Teach child to explore the message and meaning of own behavior, seeing it in a new way.	Assist child to develop her own personal agenda for healing.
• Ensuring no further abuse occurs;		
• Introducing the concept of the importance of physical and emotional "safety";	Introduce the child to the kinds of patterns, both behavioral and cognitive, that have developed and that are interfering with her well-being.	Empower child to make healthy choices, find inner strength to deal with new issues as they arise.
• Expressing an interest in the child as a whole human being, not solely as a victim of abuse.		
• Assisting the child to understand the goals and limits of the environment; and	Support child to tell her story. Provide the emotional sanctuary necessary for her to examine her perceptions of the abuse, the abuser, significant others, and herself.	Incorporate her abuse into a whole, healed self, so that the abuse no longer impacts on daily functioning.
• Creating an atmosphere where discomforts can be discussed.		
		Specific objectives:
Assess: observe, track, document significant behaviors. Prioritize intervention required to maintain placement viability.		• Overcoming fear,
		• Developing a more positive sense of self,
		• Developing a positive internal dialog,
		• Setting and maintaining personal boundaries,
Begin to understand the meaning of the child's behaviors as a form of communication.		• Experiencing satisfying interpersonal relationships,
		• Experiencing a full range of emotions without disintegrating, and
		• Establishing strong problem-solving skills.

Tasks of the Caregiver

Prestory	Story	Poststory
Develop a safe therapeutic container:	Support the child in sharing her version of the abuse.	Teach the child to acknowledge the strategies she employed to survive and the courage she demonstrates in her struggle to give up any strategies that are no longer useful.
• Thoroughly assess, document, and prioritize for intervention all presenting behaviors.	Assist the child in discovering and exploring the meaning of the abuse to who she is and what her ideas are.	
• Organize and record in a clear manner all data, significant issues, and interactions so that any existing patterns (including temporal sequencing) become readily apparent.	Support the child to construct a more objective, "real" sense of the events around the abuse.	Support the child as she processes the meaning and consequence of the choices she makes.
• Uncover the impacts of the abuse on the relationships between the child and important others in her life.	Guide the child as she uncovers the impacts of the abuse on the relationships between herself and important others in her life.	Reinforce the positive gains made and her ability to function in the world without being compelled by the script of the abuse.
Clarify family relationships, working toward eliminating any severe negative impact of contact or communication with family members (toxicity).	Introduce the concept that the abuse is not the child and that it does not need to define her. Help the child to see a possibility of redefining herself.	Educate the child on creating a positive internal dialog.

Provide practice opportunities and feedback for positive social interaction. |
Develop the therapeutic relationship:	Introduce empowerment through making choices. Begin exploration of the meaning and impact of choices.	Create practice opportunities for safe expression of powerful emotions. Assure the child that she can survive those emotions, without relying on negative behaviors.
• Provide the child with messages that she is important and valued.		
• Model how interpersonal safety, personal boundary setting, unconditional respect can lead to a nonabusive relationship.		
• Invite the child to join in the process of self-discovery.		Provide opportunities for the child to test her newly developed life skills. Provide support, modeling, and practice opportunities for positive problem solving.

Predict future areas of difficulty, including discussion of the kinds of supports that the child may need as she matures. |

Skills Required of the Caregiver

Prestory	Story	Poststory
Strong behavior management skills.	Advanced behavior management skills.	Ability to let go and allow the child to function without clinician's protection. Willingness to let the child make own decisions, even when the decisions are not always good.
Ability not to be personally affected by the child's behavior; ability to seek out support and supervision as the child tests the relationship.	Tolerance of behavioral difficulties. (As the child approaches the point of full disclosure, stress, anxiety, and fear build up so that the child appears at her worst.)	
Ability to observe, understand the meaning of, and uncover patterns in interactions and behaviors.	Superior counseling skills, with emphasis on exploration, appropriate use of language, musing and reflecting, and nonjudg-mental, neutral stance.	Ability to teach social skills, problem-solving skills, positive thinking skills (internal self-dialog). Strong reinforcement skills for positive decision making, positive problem solving, etc.
Ability to use language and concepts appropriate to the child's developmental level.	Avoid jumping to conclusions, preempting the child's own internal processing, moving at own pace instead of the child's, or investing too much in own personal reaction.	Good processing skills for exploring negative decision making, negative problem solving, etc.
Counseling skills, including active listening, reflection, open-ended questions, clarification.	Validation of the child's perceptions, ideas, thoughts, and experiences. ("What was that like for you?")	Ability to tolerate, contain, and facilitate the expression of strong emotions, both negative and positive.
Ability to tolerate and allow the child's negative and positive feelings about the child's abuser and significant others.	Posing alternative ideas for the child about the events of her life or her reactions to them. ("I wonder if ... ").	Ability to communicate positive, accepting, and non-judgmental regard for the child and ability to teach the child to honor and respect herself in a similar way.
Competent writing and organizational skills. Good team communication skills and ability to follow through on input and supervision.		
Self-awareness and the ability to maintain clinical objectivity.	Normalize the child's living experience wherever possible. (Moving the aftermath work to an "office" is an important technique. This leaves the rest of the milieu free for "living.")	Ability to tolerate setbacks and uneven growth without personalizing or becoming overly negative about the child.
Ability to communicate unconditional positive regard, respect, nonjudgmental attitude, and acceptance of the child.	Maintenance of all previously identified skills.	Launching/termination skills for children discharging or terminating from the therapeutic process.

Appendix D
House Rules about Being Safe

Our house has these rules so that everyone will know what to expect from one another and will feel safe and comfortable.

Rules about where we can go
1. These are the rooms that we can all be together in:
   - Living room,
   - Dining room, and
   - Family room.

2. For these rooms, you need to get permission from the person whose space it is, and an adult must be present (you should be able to say, "Don't come in," and have that be respected):
   - Bedrooms, and
   - Bathroom vanity area.

3. These are the rooms where you should always be private:
   - Bathroom,
   - Any place you are changing,
   - Any place you are sleeping, and
   - Any place you want to be alone in.

Rules about how we are together
1. Rules about touch:
   - No one in this house should touch another person, unless she has permission.
   - Permission should come from the person being touched and from a safe adult.
   - If a touch feels uncomfortable or unsafe, the person being touched should ask for it to stop.
   - When a touch is unsafe and uncomfortable, the person being touched should tell a safe adult right away.

2. Rules about secrets and talking:
    * There will be no secrets in this house.
    * Surprises may be OK if a safe adult gives permission.
    * Anything a person who lives in this house wants to talk about will be respected. There are no topics that are off limits or against the rules.
    * Dirty, scary, or exploitative talk is against the rules. Such talk must be reported to a safe adult right away.
    * Any time any one in this house feels unsafe or uncomfortable, she must tell an adult.

3. Rules about what we wear:
    * Everyone will wear clothes appropriate for the weather, conditions, and occasion.
    * To feel safe and comfortable, night clothes should be worn only in our rooms. If we are out of our rooms, we will wear housecoats.
    * If you are bothered by what someone is wearing, you must talk to a safe adult.
    * Private parts should always be covered. If someone's private parts are not covered, we must tell a safe adult.

Bibliography

American Psychiatric Association. (1994). *Diagnostic and Statistical Manual of Mental Disorders* (4th ed.). Washington, DC: Author.

Atkinson, W., & Zucker, K. J. (1997). *Attachment and psychopathology.* New York: Guilford Press.

Bass, E., & Davis, L. (1988). *The courage to heal.* New York: Perennial Library.

Bays, L., Freeman-Longo, R., & Hildebran, D. D. (1990). *How can I stop: Breaking my deviant cycle.* Orwell, VT: The Safer Society Press.

Bays, L., & Freeman-Longo, R. (1989). *Why did I do it again: Understanding my cycle of problem behaviors.* Orwell, VT: The Safer Society Press.

Beeler, N. G., Rycus, J. S., & Hughes, R. C. (1990). *The effects of abuse and neglect on child development: A training curriculum.* Washington, DC: Child Welfare League of America.

Berg, I. K. (1991). *Family based services: A solution focused approach.* Milwaukee, WI: BFTC Press.

Briere, J. N. (1992). *Child abuse trauma: Theory and treatment of the lasting effects.* Newbury Park, CA: Sage Publications.

Brohl, K. (1996). *Working with traumatized children.* Washington, DC: CWLA Press.

Burns, M. (1993). *Time in: A handbook for child and youth care professionals.* Toronto, Ontario: Burns-Johnston Publishing.

Butler, S. (1985). *Conspiracy of silence: The trauma of incest.* Volcano, CA: Volcano Press Inc.

Cavanagh Johnson, G., Cavanagh Johnson, E., & Cavanagh Johnson, T. (1993). *Sexualized children: Assessment and treatment of sexualized children and children who molest.* Rockville, MD: Launch Press.

Crisci, G., Lay, M., & Lowenstein, L. (1997). *Paper dolls and paper airplanes: Therapeutic exercises for sexually traumatized children.* Charlotte, NC: Kidsrights.

Davis, N. (1990). *Once upon a time: Therapeutic stories to heal abused children.* Oxon Hill, MD: Psychological Associates of Oxon Hill.

Dawson, R. (Ed.). (1986). *Child sexual abuse: Investigation and assessment*. Toronto, Ontario: Institute for the Prevention of Child Abuse.

Dawson, R. (Ed.). (1986). *Child sexual abuse: Intervention and treatment*. Toronto, Ontario: Institute for the Prevention of Child Abuse.

DeLuca, R., Boyes, D., Furer, P., Grayston, A., & Hiebert-Murphy, D. (1992). Group treatment for child sexual abuse. *Canadian Psychology, 33*, 168–175.

Donovan, D. M., & McIntyre, D. (1990). *Healing the hurt child*. New York: W. W. Norton & Co.

Durrant, M. (1993). *Residential treatment: A cooperative, competency based approach to therapy and program design*. New York: W. W. Norton & Co.

Fahlberg, Vera I. (1991). *A child's journey through placement*. Indianapolis, IN: Perspective Press.

Foster Family-Based Treatment Association. (1995). *Program standards for treatment foster care*. New York: Author.

Freeman-Longo, R., & Bays, L. (1988). *Who am I and why am I in treatment?* Orwell, VT: The Safer Society Press.

Frierich, W. N. (1991). *Casebook of sexual abuse treatment*. New York: W. W. Norton & Co.

Furniss, T. (1983). Family process in the treatment of intrafamilial child sexual abuse. *Social Casework, 64*, 263–279.

Gelles, R. J., & Strauss, M. A. (1988*). Intimate violence: The causes and consequences of abuse in the American family*. New York: Simon and Schuster.

Gil, E. (1987). *A guide for parents of young sex offenders*. Rockville, MD: Launch Press.

Gil, E. (1991). *The healing power of play*. New York: The Guilford Press.

Gil, E., & Cavanagh Johnson, T. (1993). *Sexualized children: Assessment and treatment of sexualized children and children who molest*. Rockville, MD: Launch Press.

Goldberg, S., Muir, R., & Kerr, J. (1995). *Attachment theory: Social development and clinical perspectives*. Hillsdale, NY: Analytic Press Inc.

Grand, S., & Alpert, J. A. (1993). The core trauma of incest: An object relations view. *Professional Psychology: Research and Practice, 24,* 330–334.

Hagedorn, E. (November 3, 1997). Personal interview.

Halpern, A. (April 1–20, 1994). Personal interviews.

Hawkins, R. P., & Breiling, J. (1989). *Therapeutic foster care: Critical issues.* Washington, DC: Child Welfare League of America.

Henderson, H. (November 3, 1997). Personal interview.

Hindman, J. (1989). *Just before dawn.* Ontario, OR: Alexandria Associates.

Hindman, J. (1991). *The mourning breaks: 101 "proactive" treatment strategies for breaking the trauma bonds of sexual abuse.* Ontario, OR: Alexandria Associates.

Horowitz, A. N. (1983). Guidelines for treating father daughter incest. *Social Casework, 64,* 515–524.

Jackson, K. (April 7, 1994). Personal interview.

James, B. (1989). *Treating traumatized children: New insights and creative interventions.* Lexington, MA: Lexington Books.

Kahn, T. J. (1990). *Pathways: A guided workbook for youth beginning treatment.* Orwell, VT: The Safer Society Press.

Kagan, R., & Schlosberg, S. (1989). *Families in perpetual crisis.* New York: W.W. Norton & Co.

Kimmel, H., & Gallagher, M. (August 1994). Restoring confidence and hope for the future in traumatized children: A shared responsibility of foster parents and therapists. Paper presented at the Foster Family-based Treatment Association Conference, St. Louis, Missouri.

Macaskill, C. (1991). *Adopting or fostering a sexually abused child.* London: B.T. Batsford, Ltd.

Mather, C. L., & Debye, K. E. (1994). *How long does it hurt?* San Francisco: Jossey-Bass Publications.

Meadowcroft, P., & Trout, B. A. (1990). *Troubled youth in treatment homes: A handbook of therapeutic foster care.* Washington, DC: Child Welfare League of America.

Meadowcroft, P., Tomlinson, B., & Chamberlain, P. (1994). Treatment foster care services: A research agenda for child welfare. *Child Welfare, 73,* 565–583.

Monahon, C. (1993). *Children and trauma: A parent's guide to helping children heal.* Toronto, Ontario: Maxwell MacMillan Canada.

Montgomery, M. (1991). *Children's domestic abuse program.* Charlotte, NC: Kidsrights.

Osmond, M., & Dorosh, M. E. (1992). The tri-CAS treatment foster care program: A summary of findings of a pilot project. *Ontario Association of Children's Aid Societies Journal, 36,* 18–20.

Parry, A., & Doan, R. E. (1994). *Story re-visions: Narrative therapy in the post modern world.* New York: Guilford Press.

Pescosolido, F., & Petrella, D. (1986). The development, process, and evaluation of group psychotherapy with sexually abused preschool girls. *International Journal of Group Psychotherapy, 36,* 447–469.

Redl, F. (1972). The concept of a therapeutic milieu. In G.H Weber and B.J. Haberleinn (Eds.), *Residential treatment of emotionally disturbed children.* New York: Behavioral Publications.

Rutter, M. (1975). *Helping troubled children.* New York: Plenum Press.

Schafer, H. R. (1990). *Making decisions about children: Psychological questions and answers.* Oxford, UK: Blackwell.

Sgroi, S. (1982). *Handbook of clinical intervention in child sexual abuse.* Lexington, MA: Lexington Books.

Smith, D. W., & Saunders, B. E. (1995). Personality characteristics of father/perpetrators and non-offending mothers in incest families: Individual and dyadic analysis. *Child Abuse and Neglect, 19,* 607–617.

Steen, C., & Monnette, B. (1989). *Treating adolescent sex offenders in the community.* Springfield, IL: Charles C. Thomas.

Steinhauer, P. D. (1991). *The least detrimental alternative: A systematic guide to case planning and decision making for children in care.* Toronto, Ontario: University of Toronto Press.

Steinhauer, P. D. (1993). The contribution of child treatment professionals to children served by child protection agencies. *P.R.I.S.M.E., 3,* 529–542.

Steward, M., Farquhar, L., Dicharry, D., Glick, D., & Martin, P. (1986). Group therapy: A treatment of choice for young victims of child abuse. *International Journal Group Psychotherapy, 36,* 261–277

Sturkie, K. (1983). Structured group treatment for sexually abused children. *Health and Social Work, 8,* 299-308.

Trieschman, A., Whittaker, J. K., & Brendtro, L. K. (1969). *The other 23 hours: Child care work with emotionally disturbed children in a therapeutic milieu.* New York: Aldine de Gruyter.

van der Kolk, B. (1995). *Counting the cost.* Video. Nevada City, CA: Cavalcade Productions, Inc.

Whittaker, J. K. (1979) *Caring for troubled children: Residential treatment in a community context.* San Francisco: Jossey-Bass Publishers.

Wood, M. M., & Long, N. J. (1991). *Life space intervention: Talking with children and youth in crisis.* Austin, TX: PRO-ED Inc.

About the Authors

The authors are the founders of the Treatment Foster Care Program for the Children's Aid Societies of Durham, Northumberland and Kawartha-Haliburton, in Cobourg, Ontario, Canada. The program began in 1989 as a demonstration project funded by the Ontario Ministry of Community and Social Services, and the Ontario Association of Children's Aid Societies. The program's evaluation research was published in 1992. Since then it has gone on to be one of Ontario's best-known programs among those using the treatment foster care model, and has hosted visitors from all over Canada, the United States, and even from Australia.

Most recently, the program has focused on the development of clinical protocols and training modules for treatment parents on a wide variety of topics. This book grew out of one of those protocols.

Left to right, front row: John Keating, Mary Jones (secretary); back row: Margaret Osmond, Duane Durham, Andrew Leggett.

Margaret Osmond, M.S.W., is Supervisor of the program. She holds her graduate degree from the University of Toronto and has been working for 20 years in the areas of children's mental health, family therapy, and child welfare. Author of several articles and publications on the development of treatment foster care and clinical development within the modality, she is a frequent lecturer in Canada and the United States.

Duane Durham, C.Y.W., is a Child Care Consultant, who is responsible for training, developing, and supporting a team of treatment parents. Mr. Durham holds a Child and Youth Worker diploma from Centennial College in Toronto. His 15-year career has included work in children's treatment centers as a residential worker, day treatment worker, and as a community therapist in a family preservation program.

Andrew Leggett, C.Y.W., is another Child Care Consultant responsible for treatment parent supervision. He holds a Child and Youth Worker Diploma from St. Lawrence College in Kingston. He has been a frontline residential worker and supervisor and a behavior consultant in schools. Mr. Leggett also lectures for Queen's University in the Bachelor of Education program.

John Keating, B.S.W., was formerly a Child Care Consultant with the program. He holds a Social Work degree from York University in Toronto. His experience spans a decade in frontline residential treatment, behavioral consultancy, and family work. He is currently the staff social worker on a hospital palliative care unit and a graduate student.